TO THE SUNDOWN SIDE

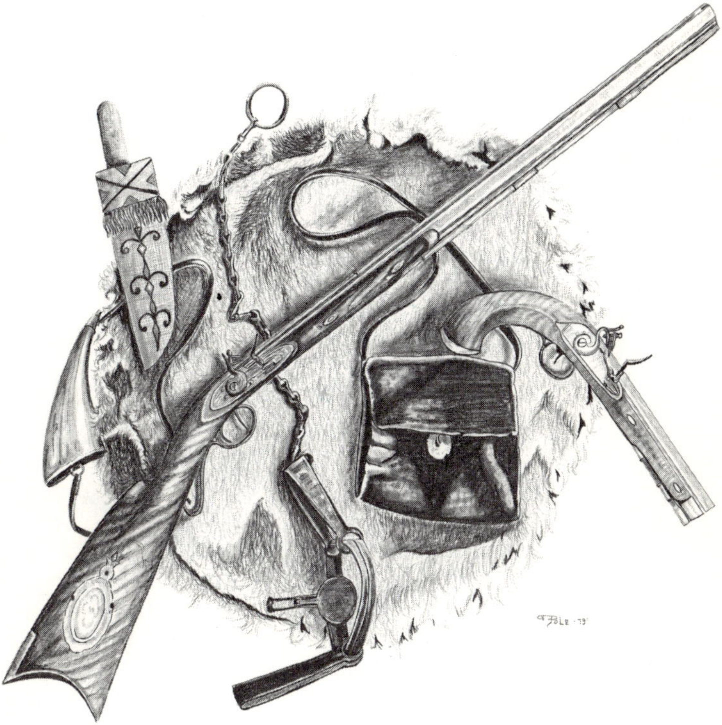

TO THE SUNDOWN SIDE
The Mountain Man in Idaho

Roland O. Byers

Illustrations & Cover
by Gregory Pole

The University Press of Idaho
A Division of
The Idaho Research Foundation, Inc.
Moscow

ISBN 0-89301-063-4
Library of Congress Catalog Card number 79-69601
Copyright © 1979 by The University Press of Idaho
All rights reserved
Manufactured in the United States of America
Printed by the University of Idaho Duplicating Services, Moscow, Idaho

Published by the University Press of Idaho — A Division of the Idaho Research
Foundation, Inc. Box 3368, University Station, Moscow, Idaho 83843

I dedicate this book
to
Sharon Kae Byers
our daughter

Acknowledgements

With sincere appreciation the writer wishes to thank the following persons who gave their expertise, time, and encouragement in the preparation of this book.

Elaine, my wife, for her lonely patience as I spent many late hours researching and preparing the manuscript.

Professor Earl Larrison, editor, I owe a considerable debt of gratitude for the many hours he spent editing the writer's sometimes disconnected phrases and without whose guidance this book would probably never have been published.

Greg Pole, accomplished artist, for his painting for the book cover and for the sketches that bring almost to life the descriptive words of the writer.

Louise Martin of Kamiah, Idaho, native American who freely gave her advice, early in the writer's search for facts concerning the history of the Nez Perce.

The library staff of the National Park Service, Jefferson National Expansion Memorial in St. Louis, Missouri, who provided the writer with a listing of research material concerning the early days of the trappers along the Missouri River.

Becky Christian, interlibrary loan librarian at the University of Idaho Library, a special thanks for her assistance in obtaining research materials from other libraries.

Also the writer's appreciation is extended to Jennifer Anderson who helped in typing the manuscript.

R.O.B.

Contents

Introduction	9
Poem, *Across the Great Divide*	12
1. Beaver Man	15
1st Interlude Philosophy of the Mountain Man	29
2. Wyakin	31
2nd Interlude The Nez Perce	46
3. Chief Black Elk	52
3rd Interlude The Appaloosa	57
4. Many Plews	61
4th Interlude The Beaver	69
5. Winterin'	72
5th Interlude The Tipi	95
6. Spring Travels	99
6th Interlude Beliefs	115
7. Pahkees	118
7th Interlude Indian Foods	129
8. Bad Medicine	133
8th Interlude Rocky Mountain Rendezvous — 1825 - 1840	140
9. Rendezvous 1826	146
9th Interlude The Indian and the Buffalo	163
10. The Buffalo Hunt	169
10th Interlude Significant Events in the Development of Trapping in the Northwestern United States	188
11. The Battle	193
11th Interlude Medicine	201
12. Vengeance is Mine	204

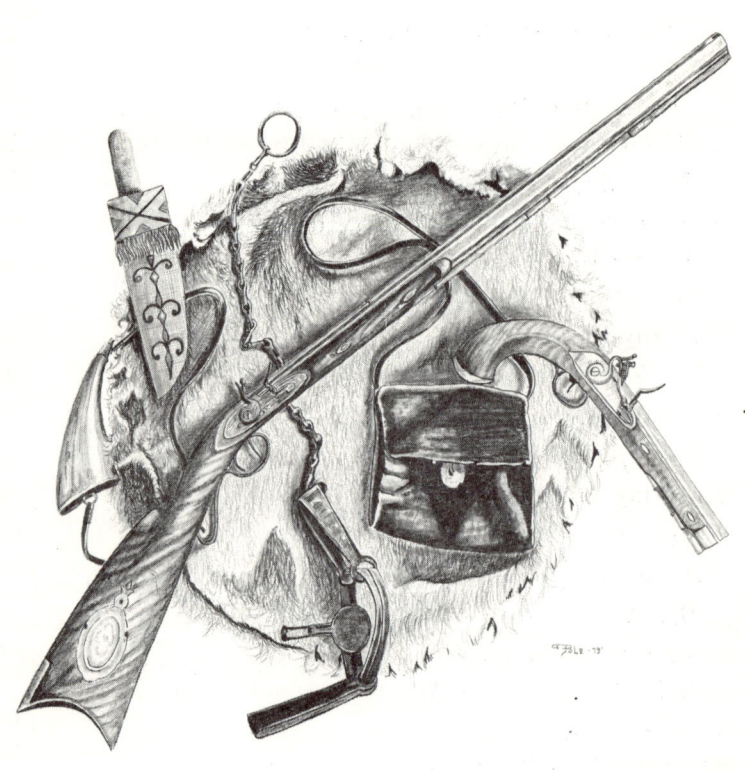

Introduction

South Pass, Wyoming — August 1975
As I stood that August evening in the fading sunlight and watched the lengthening shadows of the aspen trees extending eastward toward the approach to historic South Pass, I listened to the howl of the prairie wolf coming up from the valley of the famed Sweetwater River. The prairie wolf... the coyote... the same howl that must have caught the ear of the early travelers over this pass, a lonesome sound coming to me now from somewhere on the steep granite-strewn slope to the north.

I imagined the ghosts of the mountain men as they rode up the eastern approach to the timbered summit of the pass, with their ever-vigilant and perceptive awareness of all that went on around them . . . the flight of the birds, the movement of animals, both of their own mounts and of the wild animals. These men were always intently aware of the sounds of the wilderness, considering whether the flight of the raven was spontaneous and inquisitive, or prompted by a hostile moving through its sanctuary. They would be sniffing the air currents for unfamiliar odors of an enemy or of an animal and looking for the sign of beaver in the dam built in the stream bordering the trail, a trail that followed the sagey rise until it entered the verdant stands of shadowy evergreens that covered the east slope near the summit of the pass.

Many of these yet-to-be-tried mountain men might be faced at any moment by a band of screaming painted Blackfoot warriors who with vengeance in their hearts were willing to die with honor to keep these intruders from entering their tribal lands. The Blackfeet objected to the traders who supplied guns and ammunition to their traditional enemies, the Shoshone, Flatheads, and Kootenai. The Blackfeet had been owners of guns for many years that had been acquired in trade with the Hudson's Bay Company. With these guns, they had become rulers over much of the intermountain land of the headwaters of the Missouri, the Green, and the Snake Rivers. With superior fire power, they had forced the other Indians into the high mountain redoubts, away from their traditional homes in the valley of the Missouri. The Blackfeet had originally emigrated into the upper Missouri River country from farther north along the Bow and Saskatchewan Rivers.

The young mountain men would learn the ways of the Indian, first from the stories told by the experienced trappers — albeit colored with the individual ability of the story teller — and then, if they were fortunate, from the friendly Indians they might encounter in their travels. Sooner or later, they would be harassed and possibly even killed by the Blackfoot warriors who freely ranged the intermountain West from the Bow River in the north to the Great Salt Lake in modern-day Utah in the south.

How could I, a product of a security-minded society, envision how a man must feel when he was two months of hard riding distant from the nearest white settlement on a trail beset by dangers at every turn. Danger not only from the Indians but also from the grizzly bear, the rattlesnake, the rabid wolf, and of the heat, the cold, the thirst, the hunger, and any number of real and imagined adversaries. To know that the chance for survival was less than an even bet — to be wounded and probably die from the wound, for there were no doctors or medicine, save the Indian remedies which were probably as effective as any of the white man's medicines of that day. The psyche of the mountain man was conditioned by his frontier upbringing where life was short and fraught with danger. His was a tenuous existence, regardless of where he lived, and to ride into the unexplored regions of the mountain West must have been a challenging experience — to know that he had traveled where no other white man had ever set foot or hunkered down around a campfire.

As the darkness closed in from the east and the star-lit sky came down closer and closer, I walked back to my safe and warm home on wheels, to sleep without fear, knowing that from beyond the perimeter of a flickering campfire light would not come the scream of a hostile, the twang of a bow string, or the smoky blast of a smooth bore musket. I could not walk in the moccasins of a mountain man, for there was no common link with which I could establish an identity. I could only speculate or imagine how he must have been motivated.

Roland O. Byers

Across the Great Divide

To the sundown side of the great divide
Rode the men to trap the beaver.
They came in a tide from far and wide
In their quest to sate a fever.

Now the mountain man was kin of the clan
Whose feet were itchin' to roam
And he tried his hand at trappin' the land
In a wilderness he'd soon call home.

They followed west the men whose quest
Was a passage to la' Chine,
A search not blessed by luck's caress
But found a land serene.

Beyond the steep and hoary peaks
Lay riches seldom found
In icy creeks the pelts they'd seek
Then stretch on willow round.

The land was raw yet home to all
Whose skin was red in hue,
From whom for an awl and some foofaraw
They'd trade the beaver plew.

Men traded their plews at a rendezvous
For supplies and trapping gear
With jerky to chew and traps all new,
They were set for another year.

To the sundown side of the great divide
Rode the men to trap the beaver.
They came in a tide from far and wide
In their quest to sate a fever.

      Roland O. Byers 1977

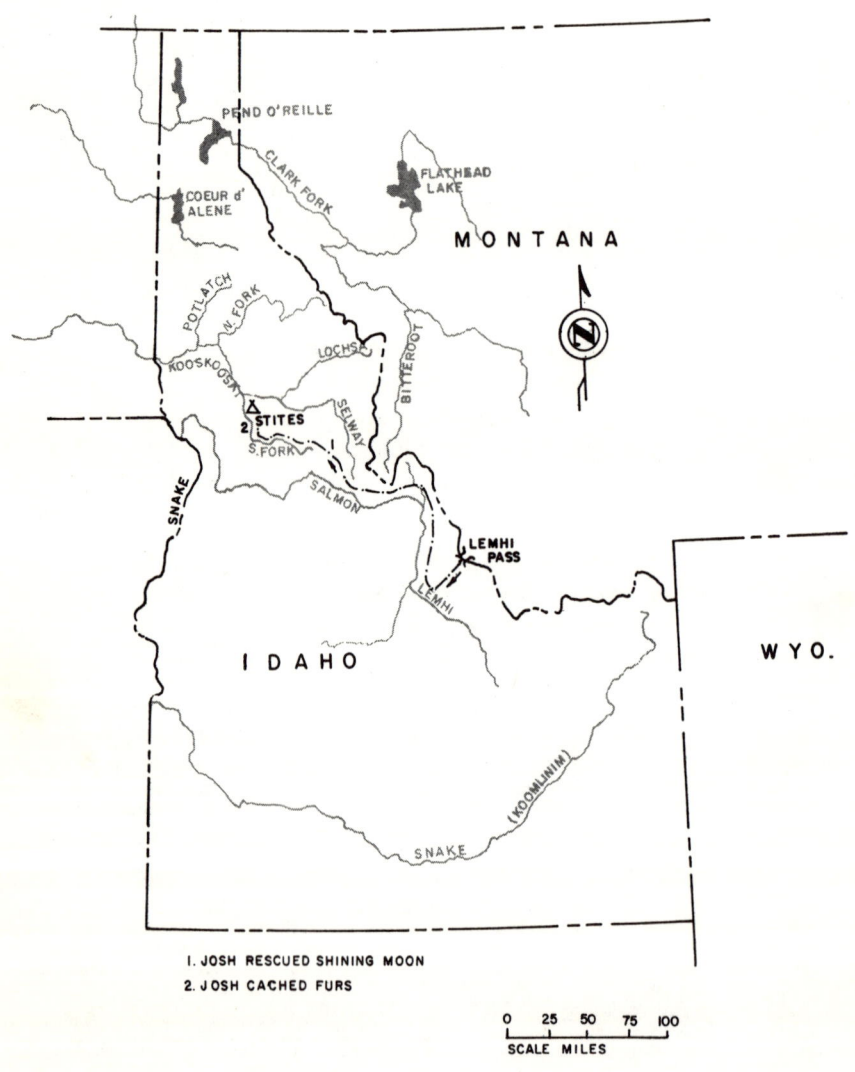

Josh's Entry into Idaho

Chapter 1
Beaver Man

It was nearing sundown on a hazy blue day late in August in the year 1825 as Josh Copeland rode westward toward the country in which he would do his winter's trapping. He was in the high country of the Bitterroot Mountains and earlier in the day had, by dint of hardness, crossed the continental divide. He stopped his pinto gelding in a clearing in the Douglas fir forest to drink in the immense panorama before him. This was his first trip into the Salmon River drainage, and as he looked to the west down the valley of Agency Creek to the Lemhi River and beyond to the Lemhi Mountain Range and beyond that to the Salmon River Mountains, he was enthralled, for such a view never ceased to strike him with awe. There is no place on earth like the high country of the West to put a man in his place. Here was a trapper's "Nirvana." Certainly, God had meant such a vista to be reserved for reverential meditation.

As he sat there sideways on his horse on one leg, so to give his buttocks a rest, his senses were shocked back to reality by the nearness of the shrill bugle of a bull elk. There is no sound in nature, except possibly the scream of a cougar, that will raise the hair on the back of your neck and tighten your sphincter like the mating call of a bull elk. It was not often that Josh indulged himself the luxury of relaxing his senses, for the penalty for such unawareness in the western wilderness is often death or, even worse, capture by the ever-present hostiles thirsting for your blood, your scalp, or the contents of your possibles bag. Looking to the .50 caliber Hawken flintlock rifle cradled in his left arm and to the priming in the pan, he squinted his deep-set blue eyes and peered into the evening sun, searching the finger ridges running down to the small alpine meadow before him. He sniffed the clear mountain air for the musky smell of elk. He was hungry for the taste of an elk tenderloin roast for next to boudins, buffalo hump, or roasted beaver tail, an elk roast was probably the best grub available to the mountain man. Three weeks had elapsed since Josh had first entered Blackfoot country and had slept in as many cold camps, for he had not wanted to betray his presence in a hostile country by firing his rifle to obtain food. Now that he was on the border of Shoshone and Nez Perce territory, he was not quite as reluctant to chance attracting attention. He had subsisted on summer berry pemmican, buffalo jerky, rainbow trout, fool hen, and berries since the first week in August when he had departed the vicinity of the fur rendezvous. That first Rocky Mountain rendezvous had been held during the first week in July and was over by the 8th. It took place on Henrys Fork a few miles above its confluence with the Green River, the "Sisk-a-dee," which General William H. Ashley had chosen for the first full-blown Rocky Mountain fur rendezvous. Jedediah Strong Smith had replaced Major Andrew Henry as Ashley's partner in the Rocky Mountain fur trade.

The past year had been one in which Copeland had trapped beaver in the country of the Blackfoot along the upper Yellowstone River and although there had been several close calls with the Indians, he had managed to keep his hair. During the past year, he had fulfilled a contract with General Ashley and Major Henry for one-half of his catch of beaver pelts in return for the supplies needed to sustain him in the mountains for the year. Josh had made a fine catch of beaver and had packed enough plews (pelts) to the rendezvous to pay off his indebtedness and to buy outright an outfit for another year of trapping. Now that he was independent of debt, he had achieved the enviable status that all mountain men strived for, to be a free trapper — to be beholden to no man. Although as a free trapper he was able to travel to any part of the West he wished, he was reluctant to return to the Yellowstone country because of the troublesome Blackfeet. They limited a trapper's range and freedom and thereby his productive lifts, plus the ever-present chance of losing his topknot. So, he decided to search for a new trapping country. While at the rendezvous, he had heard of a region beyond the Bitterroot Mountains and in the drainage of the Columbia River. It was in the land of the Nez Perce Indians, who were considered friendly to the white man. It was not only full of beaver, but he would be relatively safe from interference by Indians. To trap effectively in Blackfoot country, it was necessary that the trappers band together in large groups to discourage attack from the hostiles, who would not as a rule attack unless they felt they had a superior fighting force. This banding together by the trappers reduced the individual beaver take somewhat and the chance for discovery was greater.

He had also heard that the Nez Perces were expert in the breeding of horses and had developed a horse typified by a spotted rump, tough hooves, and good endurance, which they had named the Appaloosa. It was reputed to be a superior horse for mountain travel. Josh wanted such a horse, a dependable horse which was often the edge when only a little margin was the difference between life and death.

* * *

As the mountain man searched the area before him, an exceptionally large bull elk walked majestically into an opening in the fir on the knee of one of the finger ridges. Here was a magnificent animal with an immense seven point rack held high by an almost black head. A huge bull, it must have weighed almost half a ton. Then, the reason for that challenging bugle became apparent. A second but somewhat smaller and younger bull sounded a high-pitched and almost soprano bugle. Fretting in the rut, the bachelor bull moved into the battle arena. The young bull wanted for his own some of the cows husbanded by the black herd bull, to satisfy the paternal urge that nature had coursed through his veins, swelling the glands in his neck and pumping from his musk glands the pungent odor that hung heavy in the air.

"Well, I'll be hornswoggled," the man said as the antlers of the two bulls clashed together, and he watched in fascination the battle. Here was nature's way of deciding who was to be the father of next year's calf crop. Only the strongest and bravest were afforded the pleasures of the rut. The mountains resounded with the clamor and the air was filled with dust. The battle soon ended, however, as the young bull was a novice and no match for the experienced herd bull. The challenger was at least two years away from his prime and he judiciously retreated to fight again another day. As he turned and walked away, the big herd bull squealed in derision and turned back to his waiting herd.

The man again sniffed the air but could detect little but elk musk. He decided to try for an elk roast and plotted his course for stalking the bull and his cows. Reaching into his possibles bag, he withdrew a whistle made of elderberry bark. He would blow the whistle and "bugle the old bull up," hoping to get a close shot. Dismounting his horse, Josh glanced back at Midnight, his black pack mule, a jenny, and dropped the bridle reins in front of his horse. After checking the direction of the wind, he walked silently upwind through the subalpine and Douglas firs to the battle-scarred finger ridge. As he neared the clearing in the trees, he cocked his piece, pulled the set trigger, placed the whistle to his lips, and blew a several octave call. Almost immediately, the herd bull answered the call and came on the run, crashing through the trees, downwind toward the bugle to protect his harem from yet another intruder. A bull was not as cautious during the rut as he would usually have been. He normally would have quartered into the wind and circled the area from which the challenge came. The bull advanced into the clearing head down, mane bristling, and horns forward toward the challenger. The trapper placed a half ounce ball from his rifle into the neck of the bull, breaking his spine and dropping him in his tracks. The man then reloaded his rifle and primed the pan, watching all the time for any movement in the elk. He took a butcher knife from the sheath on his knife belt and proceeded to butcher the bull. As soon as he had gutted it out, he cut off strips of the hot steaming liver, dipped them into the ruptured gall bladder, and chewed them with relish, the elk blood running from his mouth. Grunting his satisfaction at the taste, he then cut off as much of the tenderloin and high rump meat as he could readily use and wrapped the meat in clean muslin. After cutting out the elk teeth, he returned to his horse and pack mule and packed the meat into parfleche panniers. He then resumed his travel down the trail.

By way of farewell there came a bugling sounded by the young bull who could now unopposed take over as boss of the leaderless herd. He in turn would be challenged by other bachelor bulls seeking the right to father a generation of elk.

Now that the man had fresh meat, he began to look for a camping place where there was wood, water, and grass. He would camp high up near the headwaters of Agency Creek, off the path usually taken by traveling Indians and where, if the need arose, he had only to kick over the ridge as a path of escape.

* * *

Josiah Copeland was a young man. He was twenty-five years old, but he was wise in the ways of the mountains. He had apprenticed his job, learning mountaineering from the expertise of David Jackson, William L. Sublette, and Jedediah Smith. Like all mountain men, he had been judged by others as one who was courageous above all else. It was this dauntless courage that deterred the Indians from molesting the mountain men unless they had a decided advantage in numbers or could attack from ambush. "Josh" was a big man, even in a world of big men. He stood six feet five inches in his moccasins and weighed two hundred and forty pounds, give or take five. He had come to love the West — the limitless trees standing row on row, the thirst-quenching qualities of the clear mountain stream water, the smell of sagebrush on a hot day, the glistening of the snow-crested mountains above the serenity of their verdant forests, the flash of a trout as it rose to a fallen insect, the taste of hump ribs, boudins, and roasted beaver tail. He was at home in these environs. He could shoot plumb center with his Hawken flintlock rifle and his eyesight was "nigh that of an eagle" and his sense of smell like that of the carcajou. The combination of these senses had saved his life on more than one occasion. His keen sight permitted him to detect any movement in his field of vision. He could read sign better than most Indians and tell who had passed that way, whether it was Blackfoot or Sioux, Pawnee or Crow, Teton or Cheyenne, Shoshone or Eutaw, Nez Perce or Flathead. There was not an animal that left sign that he could not identify. He could read the age of a sign within a few hours and he was proud of his own evanescent qualities. He was capable under any emergency and would without provocation kill to protect his own or the weak in any situation. He was faithful to his own code of honor.

Josh wore the clothes that best fitted his life style. His

breeches were made of tanned elk skin; a shirt and skintight undershirt, of antelope skin; leggings, of buffalo hide; and moccasins of dressed buffalo hide made from last year's tipi cover and parfleche soles. This was completed with a coat of buffalo hide and a hat of otter skin, all of which he had traded for with the Shoshone Indians. In his pack he had pieces of blanket to wrap around his feet and hands in cold weather. His hair was long about his shoulders, but his face was smooth shaven.

 The mountain man's personal equipment included two apishamores made of buffalo calf skin, one of which doubled as a saddle blanket and at night as a ground cloth for his bed, as well as a riding saddle and bridle, a buffalo skin sack in which he carried his six beaver traps, a Hudson's Bay three point blanket, two extra pairs of moccasins, a wood-stoppered powder horn made from the horn of a buffalo bull, a buffalo cowhide knife belt attached to which was a scabbard for his butcher knife, as well as a tanned deerskin possibles sack in which he carried his pipe, tobacco, elk bugle, a wood-stoppered antelope medicine horn in which he stored beaver bait (castoreum), a firebag in which were implements for making fire (flint, steel, and some dry punk), a bullet mold with brass ladle and lead for casting bullets, extra flint for his flintlock rifle, and a brace of Ketland .65 caliber flintlock horse pistols. He carried in one of his parfleche bags a rosewood flute given to him as a boy by his grandmother which, when on occasions he played it, delighted him and completely paralyzed the Indians with wonder.

 As Josh rode along the Indian trail, he was alert for a suitable overnight camp. At all times, he observed the flight of the birds and listened to the sounds of the mountains, sensing any unnatural noises and movements. He heard the raucous call of the pileated woodpecker and watched its undulating flight to a perch on a buckskin tamarack tree. After crossing some rocky ground and coming to a tributary of Agency Creek, he turned up the stream, watching the water for any unusual floating debris, until he came to a high meadow against the mountain. Here he made his camp well hidden in a thicket of willows where in case of attack he was not far below a ridge for easy escape. After unloading his pack mule, he laid out his duffle in close proximity to the level ground where he would make his bed. He unsaddled his horse and picketed both it and the mule, each on a rawhide lariat where there was abundant green grass, yet close enough to camp for him to observe their actions and movements and to be easily accessible for escape if necessary.

He then took from his firebag a flint and steel and prepared to light a fire. He selected a piece of dry punk from the bag and, finding some dry grass, twisted them together. By striking sparks with the flint and steel, he ignited the punk. He waved the punk in the air until the grass ignited and then piled larger sticks on the flame until he had a good fire burning. There was plenty of dry aspen and willow wood available with which to make a smokeless fire. As soon as the wood had burned to a good bed of coals, he spit the five-pound elk loin roast on the end of a green willow stick to broil. The willow would impart no taint to the roasting meat.

While his elk roast was cooking, he busied himself with camp chores and the making of his bed. He had selected a high level piece of ground, found a flat rock for a pillow, and placed it at the end of the bed away from the fire. Over his rock, he laid his apishamore, a tanned buffalo calf skin, for a ground cloth. On top of that, he spread a buffalo robe, tanned hair on, and over that a close-woven eight and a half pound Hudson's Bay, three point blanket. The blanket was almost impervious to water and served to shed the rain and dew as well as keep him warm in the coldest weather. He looked up at the sky and 'lowed as how it was going to be a cold night for the sky was clear and he was camped at an elevation of about 7,000 feet. There had been frost now for several nights and the leaves on the huckleberry and ninebark bushes were already turning red and the mountain maple was as golden as the sunset. He was glad to see the frost, for it reduced the numbers of mosquitoes and no-see-ums and thereby made life just a little more bearable. With his knife, he scraped a ditch around his bed to carry away the water just in case it rained during the night. This was the time of the year when, even in this dry country, it could rain or even snow. When he went to bed, he would remove his powder horn and bullet pouch that were suspended around his neck by a rawhide shoulder belt. These, along with his rifle and handguns he would lay by his side under the buffalo robe within easy reach, just in case old *Ursus horribilis*, the grizzly bear, decided to get friendly or an Indian should decide to "count coup" and try to lift his hair.

When the elk tenderloin was roasted and he had eaten all five pounds of it, he topped off the dinner with a pint of huckleberries he had picked earlier in the day. Josh mused to himself that he was living in fat times. He then took from his possibles bag a corncob pipe, which he filled with a mixture of tobacco and kinnikinnick (the inner bark of a red willow), picked up an ember from the fire, and lighted the pipe.

Puffing on the pipe, Josh blew the smoke into the air and as any prudent mountain man would do he listened to the sounds of the night: the night birds, the murmur of running water, and the horse and mule's cropping the grass. He felt the cool air moving down the draw and as he sniffed the air, he could smell the pungent odor of wet soil, the sweet tart odor of huckleberries, and the musty scent of the packrat nest under the rocks in the talus slope. As the smoke drifted up into the willows, his mind turned back to his home in Belmont County, Ohio. He had lived there with his teacher father and his mother in a small settlement just a day's walk south of Zanes Trace. After graduating from high school, he read for a time to be a lawyer. His law career, however, was cut short by the untimely death of both of his parents when they contracted smallpox. At the age of 22 and with no close relatives, he decided to seek his fortune by trapping beaver in the West. With a portion of the money he had received from the sale of his inherited property, he purchased a good riding horse and some gear and headed west for St. Louis.

St. Louis in June of 1822 was the center of activity for the American fur trade. During that summer, several brigades were known to leave for the upper reaches of the Missouri River. It was estimated that more than a thousand men were employed in trapping furs on the waters of the Missouri River. In St. Louis, Josh soon joined a brigade of trappers and headed west up the Missouri. All of this had been only a short three years ago, but it seemed to him now that he had been away from those civilized environs for a tolerably long spell.

* * *

Morning comes early in the mountains and Josh quickly assembled his gear and continued his trip down the Lemhi Valley toward the Salmon River. He came down out of the mountains on the flood plain of the valley and as he approached the Salmon River he observed a herd of antelope standing nearby, almost without fear, watching curiously his approach. He saw, too, the many golden eagles and the osprey in the valley and noted their feeding on the spawned out salmon along the shores of the river. There were silver chinook salmon and also red sockeye salmon floating in the backwaters of the river and the stench was almost more than was pleasant. "So this was the Salmon River," Josh mused to himself, the "River of No Return," that had thwarted the efforts of the Lewis and Clark Expedition in 1805 to descend its churning maelstrom to the waters of the Columbia River. They had been forced to follow the Lolo Trail down to the Kooskooski (Clearwater) River and then down Kimnoolnim (Snake) River to the Columbia and on to the Pacific Ocean. The Salmon River here seemed placid enough, Josh thought, almost belying its notoriety. He followed northward down the river, keeping well back from the water because of the chance of encountering Indians, which were much in evidence. He came to the confluence of the North Fork with the main river. Here, the Salmon turned abruptly west into the Salmon River Canyon through which the river launched itself into a tortuous and tumultuous course until it emptied into the Kimnoolnim River in the Hell's Canyon.

Josh continued up the North Fork for about five miles, climbing rapidly toward Lost Trail Pass, as named by Lewis and Clark. He continued upward until he came to an Indian trace known as the Nez Perce Trail. Sitting astride his horse, he studied the trail and observed that it was a well-worn one and had been heavily traveled within the last 48 hours. This trail had been used for many years by the Nez Perce and other western Indians going to and from the buffalo country on the eastern side of the continental divide. From here the trail followed westward the watershed between the Salmon and the Kooskooski Rivers, through the Bitterroot Mountains, to the headwaters of the South Fork of the Kooskooski. It was there in the high country he intended to spend the winter trapping.

As Josh turned up the trace, he wondered why Lewis and Clark had not followed this trail down the Pacific slope, for they had passed this place, but had continued on up over Lost Trail Pass, then down the valley of the Bitterroot River and then up Lolo Creek and over the Lolo Pass, a trip that was almost 100 miles longer and much more difficult. He not only pondered this question but also why the Shoshone Indians had not directed Lewis and Clark to the Hellgate, a distance of 11 miles from Lolo Creek and there launch boats down the Clark Fork River, a tributary of the Columbia and thence down to the Pacific Ocean. The Indians knew that the Clark Fork River was in the Pacific Coast drainage, as they traveled the water level route into the buffalo country during the winter and spring.

How did it happen that Josh, who had never taken a step west of the continental divide, know of the Nez Perce Trail and the western slope? Well, Bill Williams... "Old Hard Case"... mountain man extraordinary who had spent many years in the mountains and for years ridden an Appaloosa horse which he had gotten in a trade from the friendly Nez Perce Indians had taken a fancy to this young but astute mountain man and over an evening's campfire had told him of the country far to the north.

Josh followed the Nez Perce Trail westward for two days, passed over the Salmon River Mountains by the headwaters of Sabe Creek, a tributary which flows south into the Salmon River, and rode on along the high ridge between the Salmon and Kooskooski Rivers until he came to the vicinity of Burnt Knob. The character of the country continued to change as he rode west. The vegetation had varied from that of a relatively dry climate in the rainshadow of the high Salmon River Mountains in which grew the lodgepole pine at the high elevations with sagebrush and prickly pear cactus at the lower elevations along the Lemhi River to the lush growth nurtured by deep winter snows, a moist spring, and a cool summer. It was now a country characterized by huge ponderosa pines which grew on the south- and west-facing slopes, the Douglas fir, grand fir, white pine, and hemlock that grew on the north- and east-facing slopes, and the verdant stands of western red cedar which scraped the sky, up from the moist glades and swampy alluvial plains, swamps that came from centuries of silted-in beaver ponds.

It was here on the high ground of Burnt Knob, a mountain of some prominence well above the valley of Bargamin Creek, that he decided to spend a day or two and get his gear in shape for the fall trapping season. He had observed beaver activity in the streams he had passed along the trail and decided to rest the animals and scout the area for a trapping base. He established camp on a south-facing shoulder of Burnt Knob well above the trail where he could observe his back trail to the southeast and where he could also watch the trail as it descended westward into the Bargamin Creek valley. This was high country above 8,000 feet and he could see the surrounding area in just about all directions. He also had, if necessary, an escape route along the ridge to the north toward White Top Mountain. It was late afternoon with the sun still two hands above the horizon to the southwest. He busied himself with camp making and taking care of his animals before watching the trail for any activity. Up to now, he had not seen any Indians but had noticed large numbers of old horse tracks on the trace. He had been careful to ride beside the trail for the last mile or so as he searched for a suitable camping place, to minimize the chance for discovery.

On the following morning, after having been awakened at sunrise by a short but violent wind, Josh spent some time cleaning and preparing his equipment in readiness for fall trapping. The plews would be prime now as the fur of the beaver thickened for winter. He cut dry float sticks and thin poles and prepared and filled his horn bottle with medicine, castoreum, the bait used to tempt the beaver into the vicinity of his traps. The float stick is made from hard dry wood so that the beaver would not eat it. It is about four feet long and an inch in diameter and is tied to the ring at the end of the five-foot trap chain with a rawhide thong. The trap is set in water so that if the trapped beaver pulls the chain free from the anchor the weight of the trap will drown the animal and the float stick will show the location of the trapped beaver on the bottom of the stream. If the beaver is trapped in such a way that it can climb to dry ground, it will chew off the foot caught in the trap and escape. From this situation came the often repeated saying made by the mountain men: "That's the way your stick floats."

The scent pole, a stick about three feet long and one-half inch in diameter, is stuck into the ground over the trap with a few drops of "medicine" placed on the tip to attract the beaver into the trap. The "medicine" is made by mixing the orange-brown mushy secretion of the newly-dried perineal glands of the beaver found near the anus with animal fat and is stored in a wood-plugged horn bottle.

Josh made sure that his six five-pound traps that had cost him $20.00 in St. Louis were in perfect working order and that they were deodorized by smoking over a fire to take away the man scent. He then replaced them in the buffalo cowskin carrying bag. Although by appearance, the beaver gives the impression of not being a particularly intelligent animal, it soon learns to associate the smell of man with a trap and the mountain man took extra precautions not to leave any odor in the vicinity of the trap. Knowledge of the riparian habits of the beaver were very beneficial to a successful trapping season and Josh was an excellent student of the school.

There were two general sets that a trapper could make for beaver. One was along a stream in which there was a swift current that made it impossible for the beaver to successfully erect a dam. In such places, the beaver lives in a burrow in the bank of the stream. A set for beaver here required only placing the trap in the vicinity of the burrow and in water deep enough to drown a large 30 to 60 pound animal by the weight of the trap or an attached sack of sand. The second set is made in the typical beaver pond found far up on the headwaters of a stream which the beaver had dammed to provide adequate water for protection and deep enough to prevent the water from freezing to the bottom. The beaver would usually build a lodge composed of sticks and mud somewhere in the pool behind the dam. The entrances to this house would be under water with a tunnel running up into the dry and relatively safe living area above the water level. Traps could be placed in the runways or in open water with a thin stick stuck into the mud on which the medicine was applied and located to attract the animal to the vicinity of the trap. As the beaver is primarily a nocturnal animal, the trap was as a rule set late in the evening and was "lifted" at daylight, hopefully with a beaver in it. It was prudent to do your trapping during the time of day when the least amount of travel occurred on the trails and waterways of the mountains.

The actual trapping of the beaver was a miserable, cold, rigorous occupation and the mountain man spent many hours wading in the chilly water to set and retrieve his traps. As a result, the trapper soon developed rheumatism, as the best seasons for trapping plews were in the late fall and early spring when the water was always the coldest. Trapping the beaver was only the beginning of the work, for there was much to be done back in camp where the beaver had to be skinned and the skin stretched on a circular frame made from willow sticks. The excess fat and meat were scraped from the stretched skin and then it was hung out to dry for a few days. The plews were often cached in a hole dug in the ground, to be retrieved later and taken to a rendezvous for trading.

* * *

Josh was feeling the pangs of hunger as he had not partaken of food since he had eaten some buffalo jerky for breakfast. He grinned as he thought of the elk roast he had hoisted on a rawhide rope into the tree above his camp. He was about to prepare a cooking fire when he sensed an uneasiness in the actions of his pack mule and he noticed she was making a nose. Old Midnight was not only a dependable pack animal, she had probably the best nose for Indians in the mountains. It seemed she could sort out the odor of an Indian from all the other mountain smells. There must have been a memorable event in her past that had indelibly impressed that scent on her brain. Josh had never quite savvied the association, but it never failed. Besides being a good pack animal, a mule would follow a horse to hell and back. Josh had seen the mule raise her head and with her ears pricked forward look toward the trail to the west. He reached for his rifle which was always close at hand and glided flat-footed on silent moccasined feet through the open timber to a vantage point overlooking the trail.

He had only a short wait before he heard the staccato barking of a disturbed pine squirrel as it skittered with fluffed-out tail up a tree that stood along the trail in the direction of Bargamin Creek. Even though sounds are muffled in the forest and the source of a noise is confused by echoes, there was no doubt as to the direction from which they were coming. It was also apparent that there was a number of horses coming up the trail, as the scent of horse was heavy in the air.

A lead Indian scout soon emerged from among the trees riding a lathered pinto pony and moved rapidly up the steep trail. At a glance, Josh knew him to be a Blackfoot Indian of the Piegan tribe by the peculiar shape and color of his moccasins — the right light and the left dark — and by the way he was painted. Soon, eleven more horses came into view, on six of which were riders. It appeared to Josh that the party must be a horse raiding one. It was apparent also from the number of horses that the raid had been successful.

As the last horse, a magnificent gray Appaloosa stallion, passed Josh's vantage, he noted that the rider was not a Blackfoot warrior but, from her dress, was apparently a Nez Perce girl. Her hands were tied and she appeared to be either hurt or very tired. As she neared his vantage point, her horse jumped a washout in the trail and she fell from the horse, hitting the ground very hard. As she struggled to get up, a scar-faced Blackfoot warrior savagely jerked the head of his horse and wheeled around and dismounted near the girl. Yelling punitive language and gesturing for the girl to remount her horse, he struck her again and again with his rawhide whip as she struggled with bound hands to remount her horse.

"Damned savages," Josh hissed through his teeth as he watched the painted Blackfoot strike the girl. "Heathen Blackfoot savages have no compassion for man or beast," he thought, and empathy for the girl welled in his chest, but the number of Indians prompted him to use discretion as he silently and motionlessly moved only his eyes and watched the procession top the rise and start the descent toward Sabe Creek. It was then that a plan of rescue began to formulate in his mind. He mused to himself that one good mountain man with the element of surprise in his favor should be equal to six surprised Blackfoot warriors any day, particularly when there was a few years of revenge for lost companions and the fate of a Nez Perce girl prisoner to take into consideration.

First Interlude

Philosophy of the Mountain Man

The era of the mountain man lasted no longer than half of a single life span — from 1807 to 1843 — or thirty-six years. The event to which was attached the beginning of the age was when John Colter, a member of Lewis and Clark's brigade joined a trapping venture commanded by Manuel Lisa in 1807. The demise of the era was sounded by the loss of demand for beaver fur for the making of felt hats for men.

Why did the age of the mountain man draw to such tortuous environs men of such caliber? Was it the desire for personal freedom? Was it the desire for adventure by a man who had each day experienced privation in the normal rigors of survival on the colonial frontier? Was it the love of the outdoors? Or was it the need to satisfy one's inner being to prove that he could survive under almost intolerable conditions and demands on his person?

It was, as it has been down through the ages, the young man who became the adventurer, the mountain man. He had established few roots, was seeking adventure and a means of livelihood. Families were large on the frontier and it was usually the elder son who had the advantage of inheritance or of job security within the family. The younger children in the family were often indentured or bound to a business firm or a farm outside the family.

The fact that the mountain man became so imbued with the environment in which he had been cast and was reluctant to leave the country was incidental to the reason why he originally took up the vocation. There were few constraints and only the physical and mental ability of the individual, with a little luck thrown in, limited the actions of the mountain man. Here was a chance to break the social constraints which limited him. There were no laws save those of the individual himself, the immediate group or the Indians with whom he chose to associate, to which he had to conform.

Only those among the mountain men who exhibited exceptional sensual and physical prowess survived to tell about this most demanding vocation selected by a group of men in any recent time.

To withstand the extreme demands imposed on his person and his ingenuity to survive in a most fearsome wilderness, the mountain man soon adopted many of the ways of the indigenous Indian. Those who were part of and survived the age not only adapted but invariably improved on the ways and habits of the Indian. While the latter had the advantage of centuries of experience available to him, he was continually inhibited by the spirits he conjured up in his neolithic mind.

The Indian seldom made a move without first making "medicine" or consulting his own personal spirit world or if that did not seem adequate to sustain him, he would consult a medicine man, a shaman, a self-styled intermediary, who imposed himself between man and the spirit world — not unlike a modern-day preacher. In all of his activities, the Indian relied on dances and symbolism of many forms to exhort himself and his fellow man to action. Even with such assurance, the Indian would often stop his activity and break off an action for no other reason than the manifestation of an event which he considered to be an adverse sign. Such an event could be no more than the scream of an eagle or the clap of thunder occurring at an inopportune time.

The mountain man resorted to savagery and brutalism equal to that of the Indian. He could be a relentless killer. He often counted coup and would take a scalp without provocation. But in his own way, he was true to his own code of honor. His alertness, his ability to analyze an unusual situation, to determine why an animal was moving downwind, why foreign material floated on a stream, why a bird or a mammal sounded an alarm — his ability to ascertain why an unusual or unnatural happening preceded an event often exceeded that of an Indian.

Historians record the age of the mountain man as one of extreme hardship but one that drew into it many men who exhibited outstanding resourcefulness, abilities that are probably latent in many persons who embark on adventure but who are never called on to exhibit them.

Chapter 2
Wyakin

The Nez Perce Indian believed that the earth was his mother. It was the earth with its bounty of land and water that nourished his life, as would any mother for her young. He identified himself with all things in nature and lived with them exquisitely attuned as a brother and was as a shadow on the landscape. His was a spiritual feeling for all things in nature, whether animate or inanimate, and he reacted spiritually to such natural happenings as the death-dealing cold of winter, the exhausting and stifling heat of summer, the inundating and ravaging floods of spring, and the famine of the drought. In fact, he was so closely associated with the vagaries of the environment that his whole life was permeated with a spiritual fervor for living in harmony with his surroundings.

Although the Nez Perce Indian observed no formal religion as we know it nor conducted any organized religious ceremonies, he, like all men, felt a need for a spiritual power beyond that of his own, a "hunyawat ahkinkenekia" or high one. Because of this need, the Nez Perce did believe in the ability of and sought the advice of a shaman, a member of the tribe who exhibited spiritual powers and who professed to cure the sick by administering certain herbs and secret medicines, by singing sacred songs, and by incantations calling up the good spirits. A shaman could — so he professed — call up misfortune and illness on those who were bad. While the job of the shaman was considered prestigious, it could also be tenuous. For if one of his patients succumbed after treatment, the bereaved kin would often avenge the death by taking the life of the medicine man.

The closeness with which the Indian lived with nature was reflected in his daily habits. His own personal ability to call upon supernatural tutelary spirits, guardian forms that protected him or determined his actions, were known as his

"Wyakin." The Wyakin belief provided the individual with the power to call upon elements of nature, whether real or imagined, for assistance. The Nez Perce had an almost daily need for aid in seeking the key to survival, whether it was when he was swimming a river, stalking a deer, tracking an enemy, or trailing a wounded grizzly bear — when he felt the need for powers upon which he could call to bolster his courage and dispel his doubts. An Indian's personal Wyakin could be either a single force or a combination of forces or whatever specific identity that particular Indian placed on his own personal spirit or spirits.

The identity of the particular personal Wyakin for the individual Indian was sought early in life. The method of identification of the Wyakin was one of the most sacred and solemn spiritual experiences the young Nez Perce observed. The search for a personal Wyakin was observed by both young boys and girls and occurred usually between the ages of nine and fifteen. The Wyakin taken by the women was considered just as powerful as that of the men. The young Nez Perce child was given spiritual instruction by an elderly person who had demonstrated knowledge of the procedure for acquiring a strong Wyakin. The child would select some lonely place where he or she would establish a silent vigil and concentrate on the identity of a personal guardian. For the period of time that the child was engaged in such a silent vigil he or she was denied food or water, could have no weapons, and could contact no one during the search. It was a difficult time in the life of the young Nez Perce and only through considerable self discipline was communication with a personal spirit achieved. To establish a point of reference in the search for a Wyakin, a stone cairn was often built at the location of the vigil. By sitting near the cairn, which served as a symbol of faith, the child would attempt to establish communication with the spirit world and hope to identify it in whatever form it might reveal itself.

The symbol of the Wyakin might be a bull elk standing vigilantly on a ridge, a coyote slinking down a game trail, an eagle soaring high above the basalt rock bluffs, a grizzly bear snuffling in a burrow for the smell of a ground squirrel. It could be a blinding flash of lightning, a tumultuous wind that preceded a summer rainstorm, or a vivid rainbow after the storm. Whatever the form, the youth would hope for a sign that would course through the inner being and bind him or her emotionally forever to the tutelary spirit of the Wyakin.

The more secluded the place, the longer the fast, or the more fearsome the weather, the greater the chance that the imagination would create a situation that would induce the spiritual communication that would produce a Wyakin.

* * *

She-Whose-Face-Shines-Like-the-Moon-on-the-Water . . . Shining Moon . . . daughter of Black Elk . . . Tsimu'xtsimux Wawu'xya . . . chief of the Stites Nez Perce had departed her village located near the Red River hot springs on the morning of the second day before the full moon. Following the Nez Perce Trail, she walked steadily for three hours toward the verdant forest that covered the high mountains to the east. She had decided that the time had come for her to seek her own personal guardian spirit.

Along with other members of her tribe, she and her family had spent the hot days of the summer high in the cool mountains along the Red River near the hot springs. This was her sixteenth summer and it was time that she should embark on a sacred vigil in search of her Wyakin. Her mother, Spotted Fawn, had spent many years instructing Shining Moon in the solemnity of the occasion. She had established the restrictions within which a Wyakin could be acquired. Spotted Fawn had agreed that Shining Moon was well informed and that she was now ready to begin her search.

The family was preparing to return to winter camp in the lower valley near the confluence of the South Fork with the Middle Fork of the Kooskooski River, but it was here in the high country, the lush green land that she had come to love, that she must search for her own guardian spirit. If she achieved her goal of communicating with a spirit, she too could join the dance of the guardian spirit that was held each winter for those who had so recently acquired a Wyakin. Each would join the dancing circle and chant the cryptic songs telling of the power their Wyakin had invested in them. They would emulate the symbol of their guardian spirit by motions or by voice and thus reveal to the elders present the nature of their newly-acquired guardian spirit. They would paint themselves in a way that was suggestive of the spirit and make repetitive calls, each different, in a way that would enhance the pantomime.

All Nez Perce youth did not acquire a guardian spirit on their first attempt. As many were forced to give up their sacred vigil for reasons such as fear or homesickness, they would return to their homes without having experienced the exhaltation of a vision. It was also forbidden for a youth to pretend that a guardian spirit had been encountered. If the searcher falsely claimed to have communicated with a guardian spirit, he would for eternity suffer the enmity rather than the protection of the spirit.

* * *

Shining Moon climbed steadily upward to the east until she finally came to the mountain ridge toward which she had been walking. She had seen the place on the occasions when with her family she had ridden east of the mountains to hunt the buffalo.

Upon gaining the top of the ridge, Shining Moon sat down on a rock and rested. As she sat there, she looked to the south toward the bluish autumn depths of the deep canyon of the Salmon River. She turned her head to the north and looked into the equally deep canyon of the Selway River, one of the main tributaries of the Kooskooski River. Yes, it was here, on the watershed divide of much of the vast mountainous stronghold of the Nez Perce nation, that she would seek her Wyakin.

Her first act was to build a stone cairn which would serve as a symbol of her search, near which she would establish her sacred vigil. She spread the white elk skin which she had carried with her on the ground beneath a tall ponderosa pine tree and sat upon it to take up her vigil. The sun was now high in the sky and had just passed its zenith on this clear autumn day. Shining Moon sat in meditation, wondering what the spiritual world had in store for her. She was fearful and apprehensive that a vision would not be hers, for she knew that not every youth who ventured out in search of a guardian spirit was successful. She was certain that she did not wish to return home with her head hung down in failure. Only time would quell her apprehension.

As she sat in meditation, she was aware of the usual sounds of the forest, the chit-chit of the chipmunk, the almost purr-like clucking of the ruffed grouse, the raspy barking of the pine squirrel, the madrigal call of the mountain warbler, and the snort of a buck mule deer as he caught her scent, coupled with the almost impatient stamping of his feet. But none of these sounds appeared to play any significance in her quest.

The day progressed into evening. As the sun set over imposing Buffalo Hump, a peak which reared its treeless bald granite head into the red southwestern sky, she could only continue her vigil. As dusk faded into night, she felt the deepening cold of early September and she pulled the white elk skin more tightly about her shoulders, not only to keep her warm but to symbolically protect her from the sounds of night in the wilderness. She heard the mournful howling of itsaya'ya, the coyote, the almost woman-like scream of the cougar, and the threatening hoot of the great horned owl. She was determined in spite of these fearsome creatures of the night to continue her vigil.

Although she concentrated on the sounds of the moonlit night and they were uppermost in her mind, even being as fearsome as they were, she could not identify any one that satisfied her search. The night wore on and the need for sleep pressed down on her. Overhead, it seemed she could reach up and touch the stars as they circled the standing north star. Orion, the hunter in the southern sky, traversed the heavens from horizon to horizon in search of, but never finding, the great bear in the northern sky. She fought sleep, hoping that at any time her sacred vigil would be rewarded, but the event seemed to elude her.

Two days and as many nights elapsed from the time she had first set out on her quest for her guardian spirit and now she had almost reached the limit of her endurance. She knew that she could not prejudice her search by taking sustenance of any kind and she was becoming weak from hunger and thirst. She had had no sleep for two days and she was so exhausted that she was having trouble differentiating between the dream world and reality.

Then, just as dawn was breaking the morning of the third

day, was it her imagination or was it real? The wind began to blow with tumultous force, as in a thunderstorm, although the sky was clear! The trees in the pristine forest rocked to and fro. As she drew the white elk skin more tightly around her shoulders, her attention was attracted to the east, just as the sun came up over Salmon Mountain, and she saw sitting on a limb silhouetted against the red sun a Raven. As she stared in wonder at the occurrence, she heard it call to her and tell her that henceforth he was her guardian spirit, her Wyakin, and that through all her life — even though she encountered adversity and when it seemed that all had forsaken her, she must have good heart, have faith in herself and in Raven, and she would ultimately overcome all misfortune. Then the wind died down and the Raven flew away into the rising sun.

Shining Moon sat quietly thinking of what had just happened. Had it been real what she had just seen and heard, or was it her imagination? Then she recalled the trips she had made with her father to the falls on the Columbia River at the Dalles. There she had listened to the stories recounted around the campfires by Indians from the shores of the great sea and of the mythological stories of Raven.

They had told that Raven represented all that was good and was the basis of the ethics and customs of the Tlingit Indians who lived along the Pacific coast to the far north in the land of the glaciers, that as the Raven lived, so did they pattern their lives.

Now, it was apparent to Shining Moon that what had happened was not a dream but was apparently reality that had been visited upon her and she became exhilarated and no longer felt exhausted. The disclosure of the acquisition of a guardian spirit was now uppermost in her mind and she began planning how she would prepare for the spirit dance, what costumes and feathers she could prepare, and how she could paint herself to symbolize the Raven. She would carry mementos of Raven with her at all times as a symbol of her faith. She could call on this symbol of Raven for assistance on occasions of danger or stress. By the same token, she knew that if she violated any rule prescribed by the guardian spirit she would quite likely suffer adversity.

Shining Moon now stood up and stretched her lithe limbs

that had stiffened with inactivity and although physically weakened by fasting she felt exhilarated by her experience. As she stooped to retrieve her white elkskin robe, she was startled by the sound of brush cracking which she saw, as she turned toward the sound, was caused by two horses running rapidly toward her. On one horse was mounted a painted, scar-faced Indian which she identified by his paint and clothing as a "Pahkee" (Blackfoot) warrior. He was struggling to subdue a retreating Appaloosa stallion with a rawhide lariat around its nose. The Appaloosa horse she immediately identified as her father's favorite buffalo hunting stallion.

The warrior saw her at about the same moment that she saw him. Although her first thought was to run, she was weak from two days of fasting and knew she would not get far before he would overtake her. So she stood quietly as the Pahkee brought the stallion under control and rode up before her and stopped in a cloud of dust.

The painted scar-faced warrior dismounted from his pinto horse and walked up to Shining Moon and after leering at her, struck her across the face, as a symbol of subjection, with his rawhide quirt. In sign language he told her to hold out her hands which he tied together with a rawhide thong. He picked up the white elkskin robe and threw it across the back of the Appaloosa stallion and motioned for her to mount the horse. The stallion recognized Shining Moon as she approached, for she had ridden him on many occasions and he knickered a friendly greeting.

* * *

Six young Indians from the Hellgate Blackfoot tribe had ridden into Nez Perce country in search of Appaloosa horses. They had hopes of finding horses among the Nez Perce that would enhance their prestige and stature in their village. Horse raiding was a way of existence among the plains Indians. A horse raid could last for many days and cover many miles and was a favorite type of warfare among the Indians. To steal a horse from under the very nose of the owners necessitated stealth and extreme patience. It was taught by the elders of the tribe to the young Indian youths as part of their education and was practiced with a vengeance. The white man considered horse thievery with disgust, but to the Indian, it was a way of showing bravery and cunning. Nothing pleased the Indian more than to steal a horse from inside the camp of the owner. To "count a coup" was primal in the life of every Indian youth.

The six Blackfoot warriors had built their brush war lodge in the foothills from which they had made their reconnaissance of the Nez Perce Indian camp which was located about two miles southeast of Red River Hot Springs along Burn Creek. They had spent three days reconnoitering and had watched the camp of Chief Black Elk until they knew all the approaches to it and where the prize buffalo horses were tethered. In the evening of the night of the full moon, the six warriors made their raid on the Nez Perce herd of horses, some of which belonged to the family of Shining Moon. They slipped silently into the camp and, throwing meat to the dogs to keep them from betraying their presence, cut the rawhide picket lines and disappeared into the moonlit darkness, each with a horse. They had traveled fast during the night toward the Nez Perce Trail, knowing that as soon as the deed was discovered, the Nez Perce would pursue them with blood in their eyes and vengeance in their hearts.

Daylight was just breaking and the raiders were driving hard and fast to the east when a great wind spooked the horses and one pulled away from its captor. It was during the run to retrieve the Appaloosa stallion that the young scar-faced warrior came upon Shining Moon. The Blackfoot brave and his prisoner soon rejoined the others in the raiding party and, by a circuitous route taking some hours, hoping to confuse those who would ultimately pursue them, they eventually headed east along the Nez Perce Trail toward their homeland along the Clark Fork River east of the Bitteroot Mountains.

Sundown was near and the caravan had just topped a high ridge and dropped into the drainage of Sabe Creek when they began to think about food, water, and rest. Their horses were tired even though they had often switched mounts during the day. They had on occasion sent a scout back to watch their backtrail but he had reported no sign of pursuit. It may have been that by disguising their intended route of escape they had confused their pursuers long enough that nightfall would permit them some rest.

Just at dusk, the troop came to Salamander Creek, one of

the tributaries of the Kooskooski River and with still no apparent sign of pursuit, they decided it was safe to stop and rest for a period of time, so to recuperate themselves and their mounts. They waded down the creek bottom until they came to a green high mountain meadow and finding a side stream, they rode up it until they came to a natural amphitheater surrounded by steep hills. It provided grass for their horses and a level place for their camp. Their fire would be shielded by the hills from anyone traveling the main Nez Perce Trail.

The scar-faced youth who had captured Shining Moon motioned for her to dismount from her horse and he untied the rawhide thong from around her hands. Then, he hobbled her around the ankles with a thong which was just long enough so that she could shuffle along but could not run.

The Indians built a small fire, prepared and ate their meager meal of dried buffalo jerky which they supplemented with "bread," the strips of uncooked fat taken from the body cavity of a buffalo. As they ate, they talked of the success of their raid and of the great welcome they would receive back in their village. As time passed and the darkness deepened, they became more confident of their success and started making lewd remarks and motions to the scar-faced youth about the Nez Perce girl he had captured. He would, they chided, make her his slave to take care of his tipi and his personal desires. The scar-faced Indian ignored their taunts and gave Shining Moon some of the same food of which he had eaten. Shining Moon had sat down against a tree away from the campfire circle and watched her captors, wondering all the time how she might escape, and her thoughts reflected back to her experience of the morning with the Raven. Should she now call on her guardian spirit for aid? She wondered how she could contact him. Should she call out to him or should she await silently for his appearance? As the experience was new and she had not been instructed as to the way of such contact, she was in a quandary. She had often watched the dance of the guardian spirit and had been made aware of its value to help a person in an emergency, but now that she had a Wyakin, how did one go about using it? She could hear the voices of her captors, but she could not understand the words of the Algonquin family language spoken by Pahkee warriors. But she did understand some of the rude motions they were making and it only increased her desire to escape.

After the Indians had eaten, they selected one of the younger members of the party to stand guard over the horses and to secure the camp during the early hours of the night while the others slept. The six talked of the powerful medicine they possessed that had given them the prowess to steal the horses and escape without any loss to themselves. They talked of the war honors they would receive when they returned to their home at Hellgate along the Clark Fork River. The Indians threw apishamores on the ground and lay down on their sides with the palm of their hand against their cheek and went to sleep.

All of this activity had not gone unnoticed on a ridge above the camp as a silent figure watched all that was going on. Josh had followed the party on foot from the time they had crossed the saddle on Burnt Knob. He had trailed along well back of the group far enough so that he would not be detected but kept the caravan in sight most of the time. He was wary as he approached the high points in the trail, for he knew it was there they would leave a scout to watch their backtrail for pursuers.

Deepening dusk found Josh watching the party filing down the fork of Salamander Creek. He had climbed to the top of the ridge above the creek and observed their turning up the side creek that ran through the meadow. He approached cautiously along the off side of the ridge paralleling the stream until he came to a defile which led directly down to the amphitheater where the party had set up their camp. He sat down behind some huckleberry bushes that he used to break up his silhouette and there awaited darkness and completed his plan of rescue which included the need for the Indians to be asleep. In the fading light, Josh studied the route down through the aspen grove through which he must travel to approach the camp. He did not want to make any noise that would alert the Indians, as the success of his plan of rescue depended on complete surprise. His position on the ridge put him only about fifty yards away from the camp and he could easily hear their talking and in the firelight could read their sign language. He listened to the chiding to which the scar-faced Indian was being subjected and saw the fear in the face of the Nez Perce girl, and hate began to well up in his mind. His determination to free the girl obsessed him.

Josh was alert to the movements of the Indians as they traveled to and from the stream for water and in and out of the meadow to inspect the herd of horses. He kept count on them at all times as to their whereabouts. He had watched them build a fire and eat their meal. His own stomach was empty and he thought of the elk roast still hanging in the hemlock tree back in camp. But he reached into his possibles bag and brought forth a piece of buffalo jerky which he chewed on while he waited for the Indians to get to sleep and for the waning full moon to rise above the mountains.

The Indians made their plans for the night and Josh watched as one of the group with a trade musket in his hand walked out of the circle of firelight toward the meadow where the horses were picketed to take up his watch during the early evening hours. Josh saw the scar-faced youth walk over to the girl and throw food before her and later had seen him motion for her to go to the stream for water and to relieve herself.

Josh waited until the moon had climbed high enough in the star-studded sky to spread light over the meadow, like cream, so that he had good visibility in his approach to the camp. He mulled over alternative plans of rescue, one of which was an approach of stealth in which he would quietly slip into the camp and cut the thongs that bound the girl and steal silently away. Another plan was one by which he would take the bold way and kill all six of the braves and rescue the girl, get the horses, the Indians' scalps, and all. The odds, he felt, were about right for the latter plan. He had the advantage of surprise and when a Blackfoot Indian is taken unawares, he is a shrieking Indian and could be expected to be completely confused. There were only two muskets in the party; the rest were armed with bows and arrows. With this in mind, Josh thought of the horses that could be retrieved and if he could just pull the whole thing off, he thought to himself, this niggur would be welcome in the lodges of the Nez Perce forever. He preferred the latter of the two plans also as it afforded him a greater potential for a place to do his winter's trapping and a chance to exhibit his prowess as a mountain man to this Nez Perce maiden that he had "begun to take a liken to."

After an hour had passed, Josh looked up through the aspen trees and saw that the moonlight was sifting down through the branches. He decided it was time to make his rescue attempt. He felt for the knife in its sheath on his belt and the brace of .65 caliber Ketland flintlock horse pistols tucked in the belt on either side at his waist. In his left hand he carried "old bullshooter," his Hawken rifle. He would depend on his knife to complete the task, for there would not be time to reload any weapons.

There had been no movement in the camp for some time, and he assumed that the Indians were asleep. So, he began his approach to the camp, walking stealthily along the route he had picked, down the draw and into the clearing. He circled the camp well back away from the now flickering firelight and slowly and quietly moved toward the now visible Indian who had been placed to guard the horses and camp. The latter was resting his chin on his chest and leaning, not too alertly, against a wind-downed tree with his rifle leaning against the tree nearby. It had been a long day and as the youth had not slept the previous night, he was now very sleepy. Josh laid his rifle on the ground and silently slipped up behind the dozing Indian, quickly reached around his neck with his arm choking off any sound, and ran his knife between the Indian's ribs into the heart. He held the Indian against the tree until he felt the life drain from his body and slowly lowered the corpse to the ground. Josh then retrieved his rifle and looked for any movement in the camp. Seeing none, he walked slowly toward the circle of firelight. As he walked into the light, he glanced at the Nez Perce girl and saw that she was awake and as watchful as a cornered badger, wide eyes fixed on him. She made no movement and raised no alarm. He quietly crossed to the nearest of the five Indians who were symmetrically spaced around the fire. He grabbed the nearest one by the hair and in one quick motion cut his throat from ear to ear, before he could make any sound but the gurgling of air from his severed windpipe. His razor-sharp knife had done its job cleanly. The life blood of the Indian pumped in spurts out of the wound into the ground.

Before any of the four remaining light sleeping Indians could move, Josh had jumped astride the next youth and through his buffalo robe sunk his knife up to the hilt into his back.

By this time, the three other Indians were awake and as one raised his head, Josh shot him squarely between the eyes with one of his pistols, popping one of his eyes out on his cheek. The other two Indians jumped up. One, a heavy-set brave started shrieking as he struggled to place an arrow to his bow string, but before he could accomplish that act, Josh had shot him through the heart with his second pistol.

The surviving Blackfoot, the scar-faced Indian who had captured Shining Moon, came running at Josh with a knife in his hand, shrieking as he ran. Josh leveled his rifle at the charging Indian but when the hammer fell against the hazen, there were no sparks to ignite the powder in the pan and the gun misfired. The Indian dived at Josh and grabbed the gun from his grasp. This 'coup' so consumed the youth that he failed to follow up on his advantage over a weaponless mountain man. To take from an opponent his weapon in battle was an act of the highest honor. It was a 'hamanchkani,' which among the Blackfeet was an achievement greater than scalping a dead enemy or stealing his horse from his camp. Josh was without a weapon, so retreated to the body of the Indian he had killed with his knife and wrenched it from the body.

He then advanced toward the scar-faced Indian who, realizing he was in jeopardy, started his death song. The death song is not a preparation for the happy hunting ground but rather an incantation to one's guardian spirit to help him in a trying time and possibly prevent his death. It was a plea for assistance in an extreme emergency. The youth glanced around and saw the Nez Perce girl watching the action. Josh was not sure what the Indian warrior had in mind, but he made a move toward the girl. Before he could take two steps, the huge mountain man was upon him with the agility of a cougar and in one quick motion with his knife almost severed the head from the shoulders of the brave.

Josh then picked up his rifle and, looking at the flint, saw that it had misfired because of blood covering the flint and the hazen. He wiped the blood from the gun, poured powder into the pan, and reloaded both of the pistols he had retrieved. Then he walked to each Indian to be sure that all were dead.

Finding none alive, he methodically cut and ripped the scalp from the head of each one and stuck them into his possibles bag. He then went over to the Nez Perce girl who was now sitting up wide-eyed watching the whole ruckus. As he approached the girl, he could see fear in her face and he made signs for her not to be afraid, that he was here to help her.

As the girl stood up and the bright moonlight shone on her face, Josh saw that before him stood the most beautiful Indian woman he had ever seen. She was slender with narrow hips but with large, high-placed breasts. She had an aquiline nose and large, widely-spaced, almost black eyes that looked like limpid pools of black velvet. Her hair was midnight black and parted in the middle, and was plaited into braids on each side of her face and was without ornament. Her features were delicate with typical Indian high cheek bones and an almost heart-shaped face. She was dressed in a skirt of white bighorn sheep skin that reached to her ankles about which was tied a belt at the waist. The skirt was ornamented with quilled brass, beads, shells, and small bones. In spite of her ordeal and her obvious exhaustion, she stirred the passions in his body as no other woman had ever done before.

Josh cut the girl's rawhide bonds and made sign for her to follow him. She picked up her white elk skin robe and they walked to where the horses were picketed. He looped a rawhide rein around the lower jaw of a bald-faced roan horse, did the same for the Appaloosa stallion, and handed the rein to Shining Moon. He then cut the hobbles, untied the picket lines of all the horses, and stuffed the lines into his possibles bag. He mounted his horse and in the light of the full moon headed the horses down the creek and toward his camp on Burnt Knob. As they rode away from the meadow, Shining Moon was aware of a Raven flying across the amphitheater and landing in a tall hemlock tree. Her thoughts went back to the events of the day that had started at daylight and again she wondered at the occurrence.

Second Interlude
The Nez Perce

By 1825, the white man certainly was no stranger to the Nez Perce Indians. Twenty years previously, the Lewis and Clark Expedition had visited the land of the Nez Perce in making the overland trip to the Pacific Ocean. They had made a favorable impression on the tribe which was eager and desirous of cultivating the friendship of the white man. The motive for their friendship was the desire for the guns which the white man possessed and for the other trade goods that to them were so powerful. They had acquired their first guns from the Hidatsa Indians earlier in the year 1805 when three Nez Perce of the Broken Arms band from Kamiah had traveled eastward to the Middle Missouri River country and returned with six Northwest Trade Guns (sometimes referred to as the Hudsons Bay Fuzees). On their return trip eastward in 1806, Lewis and Clark had given to their Nez Perce guides two more rifles to fulfill the promise they had made on their westward trip in 1805. At that time, they had given their guides one rifle with a promise of two more. They also gave Chief Twisted Hair a rifle, powder, and 100 lead balls in return for his caring for their horses. The rifles given to the Nez Perce were U.S. rifles model 1803, one of which had been ruptured and sawed off and filed but which still shot tolerably well.

The Nez Perce visualized the visits by the explorers as forerunners of more trips by other traders and hopefully from whom they could acquire additional guns and trade goods.

Within three to five years after the Lewis and Clark Expedition, the North West Company of Montreal, Canada established trading posts on the fringes of the Nez Perce country which the Indians had visited. In 1807, David Thompson, a partner of the North West Company, established Kootenae House on Windermere Lake on the upper reaches of the Columbia River north of the present-day state of Montana. He spent the 1807-08 winter there and two years later in 1809 he founded Kullyspell House on the east side of Lake Pend Oreille in northern Idaho near the present-day town of Hope. The Nez Perce traded at Kullyspell House and also at Saleesh House which was established by Thompson in November, 1809 on the Clark Fork River northwest of Hellgate, Montana. Spokane House, ten miles from the present-day city of Spokane, was established on the Spokane River in northeast Washington in the winter of 1810-11 by Finan McDonald and Jaco Finlay, also of the North West Company.

In 1812, a post was founded in the heart of the Nez Perce country by Donald McKenzie of John Jacob Astor's Pacific Fur Company at the confluence of the Kooskooski (Clearwater) and Kimnoolnim (Snake) rivers. This post was operated for only a short time, as the Astorians of the Pacific Fur Company sold out to the North West Company after threats of takeover by the English of the latter organization during the War of 1812.

The Nez Perce were friendly to the white man. They were considered by the whites to be an intelligent and honest people, industrious and cheerful, but reticent and reserved and possessed of a dignified and proud bearing. William Clark had written that the Nez Perce were the most hospitable of any Indian nation or tribe west of the Rocky Mountains. Clark also wrote that they were fond of gambling, shooting arrows at targets, and horseback riding. They were expert marksmen, both with bows and arrows and with guns, and they were good horsemen.

During the winter of 1811-12, the Nez Perce had guided Donald McKenzie, John Reed, and Robert McClellan and eight companions out of the Hells Canyon of the Kimnoolnim over the Little Salmon River Mountains to the Kooskooski River. These men were members of the ill-fated overland expedition of John Jacob Astor's Pacific Fur Company led by Wilson Price Hunt on the trip from St. Louis to the Pacific Ocean. Besieged by hunger while traveling through southern Idaho along the Snake River, the expedition separated into small groups each of which was sent out by Hunt to try to locate Indians and trade for food. If they were successful in finding food, they were to return to the river and locate the other members of the expedition. Otherwise, they were to continue on down the Snake to find the other members of the brigade, and continue to the Columbia River.

McKenzie and his party crossed the lava fields of southern Idaho and, finding no large quantity of food, continued on to Hells Canyon which they considered to be impassable. They retraced their steps southward up the river until they found a band of Nez Perce camped near the mouth of the Weiser River. The Indians volunteered to guide the party over the Little Salmon River Mountains and down the Little Salmon River to the main Salmon River and from there to the confluence of the Snake and thence to its juncture with the Kooskooski (Clearwater) River. There, they built dugout canoes and traveled down the Snake to the Columbia. Along the way near the mouth of the John Day River, they picked up other members of the expedition, Crooks, Day, and the remainder of the brigade who had traveled overland through the Blue Mountains until they had come to the Columbia. All reached Fort Astoria in January of 1812.

These men were the remnants of the overland half of the twin expeditions, the other half of which went by sea, arriving at the mouth of the Columbia River in the ship *Tonquin* in March, 1811 and there had established Fort Astoria for the Pacific Fur Company.

During the summer of 1812, the Pacific Fur Company also founded trading posts in and on the fringes of the Nez Perce country, one of which was at the confluence of the Okanogan and Columbia rivers. Another, Fort Spokane, located somewhat nearer to the Nez Perce homeland, was established near the Spokane House of the North West Fur Company. A third post, as we have mentioned, was located by Donald McKenzie at the junction of the Kooskooski and Snake rivers across from present-day Lewiston and in the heart of the Nez Perce nation.

These Pacific Fur Company posts were productive for only one year. The threat by the British because of the war of 1812 forced the sale of Astor's Northwest holdings to the British North West Company at a price of about one-tenth of their value. This, in spite of the fact that at no time was there any actual violence between the two fur companies. However, the

British let it be known that warships were to appear at the mouth of the Columbia at any time and would undoubtedly blow any American holdings off the map.

The period between the demise of the ill-fated thrust into the Oregon country in 1811-12 by Astor's Pacific Fur Company and General William Henry Ashley's move into the high mountain country along the Green River, the Siskadee, in western Wyoming was dominated by the British North West Company and later the Hudsons Bay Company after 1821 when the two rival companies consolidated. There were only a few relatively feeble attempts by the Americans to trap the high Rocky Mountains until the Ashley interests sent Major Andrew Henry in 1823 into the upper reaches of the Missouri River where he was to establish a base of operations.

By 1825, there was such an influx of American mountain men into the Rockies that it was only a matter of time until they eventually pushed the British out of the productive trapping areas of the Rocky Mountains.

Ashley operated in a different manner than those who had previously trapped the mountains. He proposed that instead of depending upon the Indians to trap and then trade the furs to the white traders at an established fort, he would employ white men as free agents for the actual trapping. Ashley would substitute an annual rendezvous for the trading posts, transporting supplies to the rendezvous each year. These would be traded to the mountain men for their furs at what turned out to be a tremendous markup, sometimes as much as 2,000 percent for some items.

It was these mountain men who established the most significant trade with the Nez Perce, as the latter liked the informal way the Americans conducted their trade. They got along well together and the Nez Perce often guided the mountain men to the better trapping areas in their country.

The white man existed effectively in the environment of the Indian because of his superior cultural background. He was not greatly inhibited by the superstitions and traditions that plagued the Indian. Also, the white man brought to the wilderness guns, knives, traps — products of iron which were superior to the equipment possessed by the Indian and which enabled him to survive in the hostile environment with less difficulty than was the case with the Indian. While the white man adopted many of the habits of the Indian, he invariably improved on them and utilized them to his own advantage.

The Indian had developed many different languages and dialects, due in part to the relatively localized nature of his habitat. Languages were established before the Indian acquired the horse as a means of transportation and when his sphere of influence was relatively localized. With the acquisition of the horse, the Indian traveled widely and to surmount the language difference between tribes the sign language was utilized by all Indians to communicate with each other and was later learned by the white man. The Indian was a great student of human nature and read in the face of his conversant much of what was intended by the discussion. The first white men to contact the Indian in a given geographic locality had little difficulty communicating with him, even though the spoken language was different. Whether or not the Indian interpreted the intent of the conversation the same as did the white man was, of course, subject to conjecture.

Over the centuries, the Nez Perce Indians had developed a civilization relatively superior to that of many other Indians in the inter-mountain west. This superiority was probably due to the availability of ample amounts of food, clothing, and shelter which was available almost for the taking without expenditure of a great amount of effort. There resulted a source of leisure time which permitted these people to seek a better way of performing their tasks and thus improving their existence. They, in time, became the dominant nation in the inter-mountain plateau area, an area which included the country from the high Bitterroot Mountains in the east to the Dalles of the Columbia in the west and from the great lakes in northern Idaho to the Salmon River in the south.

The climate of the western slope of the Rocky Mountain valleys was relatively mild, tempered by the flow of air from over the Pacific Ocean, and did not inhibit the movement of the peoples in any season. The pre-Columbian Indian lacked an animal of any size to serve as a beast of burden or to transport the Indian himself. The woman in the society of the Indian had over the centuries suffered the greatest from this lack of means of transport for she was the one who carried the heavy load and did much of the hard work. The lack of a suitable beast of burden did not, however, limit the travels of the Indian for he is known to have journeyed on foot for long distances. He utilized the canoe for much of his travels for he lived most of his life by the natural water courses and often went to traditional trading centers by this means.

The Indian took up residence along the natural water courses because these streams provided him with a replenished source of food, the salmon and the steelhead, while the water also provided a place to float a canoe, a dug-out or burned-out tree, as a means of transporting himself and his trade goods to a trading center.

Chapter 3
Chief Black Elk

Early morning found Josh and Shining Moon on the trail herding the recovered stolen Nez Perce horses as well as the six Blackfoot mounts westward toward Bargamin Creek. The Nez Perce girl was leading the way, riding the spirited Appaloosa stallion with Josh bringing up the rear on his pinto gelding and leading Midnight, the pack mule.

Josh anticipated meeting sooner or later a Nez Perce war party which would be searching for the stolen horses. Discretion told him to place Shining Moon out in front of the string to quell any action that might inadvertently be taken by the aroused Nez Perce warriors. The herd had just crossed Bargamin Creek at Poet Camp where they had stopped to allow the horses to drink when Josh noted old Midnight with her head up alert with ears thrust forward, focusing her attention in the direction of the trail to the west. Josh looked to the prime in his guns and rode to the rear of the herd so the horses were between him and any possible attack, alertly awaiting any eventuality. He did not have long to wait, for soon in a cloud of dust, riding hard down the trail with horses lathered, came a war party of about twenty warriors. They had untangled the puzzling trail made by the Pahkee horse raiding party that had been perpetrated to confuse any one who attempted to follow the trail and try to retrieve the stolen horses. But where one horse and rider might have escaped, the many horses made a trail that had been deciphered without much difficulty. As the Nez Perce came upon the herd, first the two scouts and then the main body of Indians, they circled the horses and menacingly eyed Josh, holding their flintlock Northwest trade guns at ready. Any violent action, however, was prevented by the actions and caution of the Nez Perce maiden. When Shining Moon recognized the members of the war party to be of her tribe, she was ecstatic and slid from her horse and ran up to a tall, stern-looking warrior riding a beautiful almost white Appaloosa stallion — a man who was the obvious leader of the party.

All the members of the party were clothed in breech clouts, moccasins, and war regalia. They, as well as their horses were heavily painted for battle. Red and yellow paint was smeared solidly on the forehead of each warrior in various patterns as a symbol of strength and a red stripe was spread down the part in their hair. The guardian spirit of each warrior was represented by lines and dots of yellow, red, and green to cover the cheeks, eyelids, and body of each in various patterns.

Some of the warriors wore war bonnets made of eagle feathers similar to, and copied from, those traditionally worn by the plains Indians. The Nez Perce had copied many of the ways of the plains Indians, probably more so than any other western slope Indian nation. Others of the party wore headdresses made from the heads of buffalo, wolf, bear, and cougar, each of which held some significant place in their spiritual lives.

Many wore necklaces, armbands, and sashes fashioned from the teeth of elk, the claws of bear, feathers of birds, and strips of ermine and otter, each denoting their particular rank or the coups each had counted in his lifetime.

Each warrior carried either a gun or a bow and arrows and around his neck on a shoulder belt hung a Medicine bag in which he carried amulets and symbols of his particular Wyakin and was his own personal medicine. Each had a fire bag in which he carried flint and steel. Those with guns carried powder horns and shot.

After Shining Moon had completed the explanation of her ordeal to her father, he dismounted from his Appaloosa stallion and with Shining Moon at his side walked over to Josh. The mountain man had dismounted and loosened the girth on his saddle and stood beside his horse watching the encounter. In sign language, the Indian motioned for Josh to follow him. He walked over to his horse, took the apishamore from its back and laid it on the ground and sat upon it. He took from his Medicine bag a red sandstone pipe carved in the shape of the head of a bighorn sheep. Filling it with a mixture of tobacco and kinnikinnick, he made a sign for Josh to sit beside him on the apishamore.

Chief Black Elk lit the pipe with his flint and steel and in the traditional ritual of the pipe, touched the heel of the bowl on the ground, then in the direction of the four cardinal points of the compass, and finally to the sun and to other unknown spirits, chanting as he did his reverence to his own Wyakin, the Black Elk. The chief took a long pull of smoke from the pipe and blew it on the stem of the pipe, then in turn he handed the pipe to Josh who duplicated the ritual and as he had no guardian spirit, he related to his own religion that his mother had instilled in him all those many years ago.

During the ceremony, Josh was aware of Shining Moon as she stood behind her father watching the ceremony of the smoking of the pipe. The heart in his chest beat a little faster as he felt her black eyes on his face and it stirred in him a desire for this Nez Perce woman.

After the smoking ceremony was completed, Black Elk looked at Josh and spoke:

> I, Black Elk, Chief of the Chopunnish (Nez Perce) and the father of Shining Moon, do from where I now sit say that my heart is good. Hear me, for I am now as the eagle that soars high in the sky. Four days ago, my heart was sick as I feared the loss of my eldest daughter. She, Shining Moon, departed our village in search of her guardian spirit which she now says she has found. She tells of her capture by the Pahkee war party and how through your bravery, she was saved from a life of slavery among the Pahkee.
>
> For this and for the return of the horses, I say now my heart is good. What can I do for you, oh Long Knife, that would show that my heart is good? I cannot give you the blue of the sky or the red of the sunset, the warmth of the sun or the freedom of the breeze, for they are not mine to give. Then what in all this land can I give one so brave to show as a token of this goodness? I have little other than my own life and the lives of my family. Of them and of my worldly goods I lay before you. Take of them what you may. Of my worldly goods my horses are many and since the days of my father's father, we have been the owners of horses. We now live in a better manner

because of these horses. We now travel from horizon to horizon in search of our food. We hunt the buffalo beyond the mountains to the rising sun for our winter's food. Because of these fine horses, like those that were stolen by the Pahkees, the young and the very old now have food to sustain them through the winter until the time of the salmon in the Kooskooski River.

In return for your bravery, I give to you the spotted gray stallion on which Shining Moon rode to freedom. I have ridden this horse on many trails. It will hunt the buffalo as does no other horse, close to the side of the buffalo bull until your moccasin touches his back and into which you can drive an arrow that will pierce his heart.

Where on earth can you find a brother upon whom you can place your trust as you do a horse? It will carry you over the highest mountains, swim the deepest rivers and ask for little but green grass and a drink of cool water.

We of the Chopunnish also welcome you to the land of their fathers, a land of high mountains, shining lakes, and rivers of clear water. You will always be welcome in the lodges of the Chopunnish.

We will show you where live taxts polya'ya, the beaver that are as many as are the stars in the sky. It is good that you should ride with the Chopunnish as a brother. So that all Chopunnish will recognize you as a brother, you should always wear this string of elk teeth and bear claws around your neck.

In sign language, Josh acknowledged the magnanimity of Black Elk, saying that his life would now be as full as there are needles on a pine tree, that he would always speak well of the Chopunnish when in council with other men whether white or red. For he had found them to be worthy of the reputation given them by the two American explorers, Lewis and Clark, that of being the most intelligent and friendly Indians they had met on their westward journey.

He also thanked Black Elk for the permission to trap beaver in the land of the Chopunnish for he knew that they considered the animals of the land, the fish in the streams, the birds in the sky to be their brothers and he realized the significance of these animals in the livelihood of the Chopunnish. The Appaloosa stallion was to him a gift of greater value than any of his possesions, even 'old bullshooter,' his rifle. He would always search for green grass and cool, clear water for the horse, for to be the owner of such an animal was an honor of incomparable value.

The Nez Perce chief told Josh about the country in the direction of the Great Bear in the sky and toward the setting sun. If he would from here, follow up the Bargamin Creek drainage to its source and drop over the divide, he would be in the upper reaches of Meadow Creek which was a tributary of the Selway River, the river of quiet waters. The Selway River joined the waters of the Lochsa River, the river of tumbling water, to form the middle fork of the Kooskooski River. The Kooskooski River was the life line of the Nez Perce nation. If he would then follow Meadow Creek toward the setting sun over the divide into Soda Creek, a tributary of Red River, down which he could travel until it brought him to the South Fork of the Kooskooski River, he would then find the tribe of Black Elk in winter camp at Stites.

Josh told the Nez Perce that he would trap these waters during the fall and early winter and when the snow and ice forced him out of this country and the beaver into its lodge for the winter, he would travel the trail to the village at Stites and winter with the Nez Perce.

Josh watched the Indians as they departed, with Shining Moon riding astride a pinto pony and following closely behind her father, Black Elk. He wondered as she traveled down the trail if she, a Nez Perce Indian, felt for him as he did for her in the short time that he had known her. As Josh watched her approach the turn in the trail that would take her out of his line of sight, he saw her turn in the saddle and look back toward him. Again he wondered if she was looking at him or at the magnificent stallion at the end of the rope in his hand. He felt a tightening in his chest as she disappeared unlike any he had ever known before and he knew that some day again he must seek out this beautiful Indian woman and make her his mate.

Third Interlude
The Appaloosa

Only in recent times, has the spotted horse been given the name of Appaloosa. Throughout literature it has been considered to be indigenous to the homeland of the Nez Perce Indian, although it actually has been known world-wide for many centuries.

The Appaloosa derived its name from that given to the country of its identifiable American origin by the early French Canadian fur trappers of the North West and Hudson's Bay Companies who called the country the Palouse, a land of lush grass and abundant water.

The spotted horse raised by the Nez Perce and later owned by the white man was called "a palousey horse," a name that eventually evolved into Appaloosa. Not all spotted horses of the world exhibit the peculiar characteristics of the Appaloosa horse. The animal bred by the Nez Perce is readily identifiable by the light-colored blanket on the rump in which there are spots and flecks both in the hair and on the hide that are darker in color than is the blanket. Other characteristics include the white sclera encircling the eye, the multi-colored skin around the nostrils, and the multi-colored, vertically striated hooves. To this latter peculiarity is attributed the resistance of the Appaloosa hoof to breakage on rocky and rough ground.

The Appaloosa horse was traded to the Nez Perce Indians early in the 18th century, probably around the year 1710 by the Shoshone Indians who lived in the Boise Valley of southwest Idaho. There were natural trade routes south through the central Idaho highlands to the Boise Valley along which the Nez Perce maintained regular trade with the Shoshone Indians. It was over these trade routes that the Nez Perce first made their trips south to trade with the Shoshones for horses with strings of dentalia, the money of the Northwest Indians.

The Shoshone Indians had obtained the horses from their neighbors to the south, the Eutah Indians, about the year 1690,

who in turn had traded for horses from their more southern neighbors, the Apaches. They in turn had obtained them from the Pueblo Indians who had taken them from the Spanish settlers who had originally brought them to the Rio Grande Valley.

As early as 1521, the Spanish conquistadores had shipped many horses to the New World. Among these horses were large numbers of spotted ones which were descendants of the Andalusian horses of Spain. The first horses that came to the Nez Perce were probably descendants of the horses brought to the New Mexico area by Juan de Onate in 1598, when he and other settlers moved into the upper reaches of the Rio Grande River. This land taken over by the Spanish had been the homeland of the Pueblo Indians.

The Spanish subjugated the sedentary Pueblo Indians and used them as slaves to farm the land they once had freely inhabited. The Indians suffered under this slavery for 82 years but during the year 1680, under the leadership of a shaman by the name of Pope, the Indians all through New Mexico rose up and attacked their Spanish enslavers, killing over 400 of them. A large number of the Spanish escaped to El Paso but they had lost all of their possessions including many hundreds of horses as well as many sheep and cattle.

The sedentary Pueblo Indians had little use for horses but did keep many of the sheep and cattle. They soon traded most of the horses to other Indians who lived near them, who in turn traded these animals to other Indians, thus many natives soon came to be the fortunate owners of a means of transportation which they had never before known.

The Spanish had always forbidden their slaves, the Pueblo Indians, to ride the horses with which they had worked for many years. However, a few Indians who had been assigned to work with cattle had on occasion been called upon to assist in the roundup and were at that event permitted to ride.

To the Indians of the plains who subsisted on a buffalo economy, the horse brought about a great change in their living habits. They soon exhibited a great desire for many horses, for the mounted Indian was now relatively on equal terms with the buffalo. He could train his horse to run with the buffalo and to carry its rider so close to the buffalo that his foot touched the heaving side of the stampeding animal. With a strong bow, he could shoot an arrow almost through its body. The Indian was no longer forced to carry limited amounts of food home to his tipi by his own strength. He could dry and preserve large amounts of food and pack it on his horses often far across the mountains to his home.

With the horse, the Indian could also range many more miles throughout the country in search of food. Only the weather and other Indians limited his movements. The nomadic life of the plains Indian was greatly enhanced by the horse, as it served in many ways to free the Indian of arduous toil and drudgery. Certainly, it relieved the Indian women of much of the backbreaking labor which had been thrust on them for many centuries.

The living quarters of the Indians, the tipi, was improved because of the horse, as more and larger lodge poles and many more buffalo hides could now be transported. A large tipi might be composed of 22 lodgepoles and five buffalo hides. The lives of the young and the very old were also improved, as they could now move about on horseback, rather than walking the many miles when the nomadic Indians made their frequent moves.

The Indian possession and use of the horse developed faster west of the Rockies than it did to the east. The lands to the east afforded a minimum of good pasture and the Indians who obtained horses soon traded their excess animals away for food and other desirable trade goods. Conversely, the Indians west of the mountains had almost unlimited pasture and as the horse soon became a symbol of wealth, they were reluctant to part with any of their horses. As a result, the Nez Perce Indians obtained horses nearly forty years earlier than did many of the northern plains tribes, the Sioux, the Mandan, and the Hidatsa.

Chapter 4
Many Plews

Josiah Copeland had been drawn to the West by the beckoning call of "beaver" and led into the matrix that so imbued him with the elements that make up a mountain man that he, like many others, would never give up the life that it involved. Here he was in the most beautiful country in the world over which very few white men had ever trod, within which the Indian had lived for many centuries but who had taken from it only that which he needed for a relatively meager existence. The Indian polluted no water, cut only the meager amounts of timber from the hills that was needed to warm himself in the winter and to support his dismountable shelter. He built very few permanent structures that would deface nature's facade. He above all lived within the environment as a brother, for it was sacred to him and he treated it spiritually. He made few changes in nature that were not almost immediately reversible — "for the nomad builds no memorials."

Josh was enamoured by this existence and now Black Elk had given him the privilege of spending the winter trapping in a country that was relatively untouched by trap and gun. He would, as did the Indian, take from the country only beaver enough which he felt necessary to sustain himself for the year. In no one place would he catch more animals than could be replaced in a short time.

Josh soon located copious beaver habitat. As day followed day into the deepening winter and as each day became colder than the one before, he trapped the virgin country and had no interference from the Indians or competition from other trappers. He remained, however, alert to the capricious ways of nature for he was alone in a hostile environment where only one small mistake could cost him his life. He skinned out his beaver well away from his camps so that the carcasses would

not attract the grizzly bear, the cougar, or the wolverine, as the carcass of any animal was always an attraction to the carnivores. He would for his own use often take to his camp the tail of the beaver which when roasted would often make his dinner.

To skin a beaver, a cut was made down the belly and up the inside of each leg. A cut was made around each leg just above the feet and the feet removed. A further cut was made around the tail which was left with the carcass unless taken for food. The pelt was then removed and any excess fat or flesh scraped off. The skin was then stretched round on a willow hoop with the edges sewn to the hoop by sinew, spruce root, or rawhide thong. The round pelt was then dried for two or three days. The dried "plew" was then marked for identification and folded "fur in" and packed in bundles.

The work of trapping was cold and exhausting, for traps were set in the water late in the evening just before dark and lifted early in the morning just at daylight. The beaver is essentially a nocturnal animal and most of its activity in search of food and in dam building are carried on during the evening and night hours. Also it is prudent in the life of the mountain man trapping in Indian country to be doing your work during the time of day when the man or animal that would thirst for your blood are least liable to be on the move.

In this high country of the Bitterroot Mountains, Josh began each day just as dawn was pushing back the veil of night — a time of day that was to him one of the most beautiful of all, for each night nature lay a sparkling white carpet of lace across the high mountain meadows, a frost that turned the verdant green of summer into the metallic gold, copper, and silver of autumn, a frost soon to be evaporated into fog by the heat of the ever-lowering winter sun. His first act in the morning was to peer out from under his bed covering and look at his horses and at Midnight, the pack mule, all of which were picketed close at hand for quick access if need be. It was more propitious to count a horse's ribs than to count his tracks. He sniffed the morning air, noted the direction of the wind, and listened to the sounds of dawn so as to determine the nature of his companions, whether they be friendly or unfriendly.

Upon arising, he took from his bed his Hawken rifle, his

hand guns, his fire bag, powder horn, and possibles bag and placed the belts over his shoulder, shoved a piece of buffalo jerky from his possibles bag into his mouth, moved his stock out into the nearby meadow where they could forage for food, and then moved off upstream to inspect his trapline.

For the previous two nights, Josh had located his camp not far from a series of beaver dams along one of the upper tributaries of Meadow Creek. Today, he would move his camp over the ridge to the west to another series of dams on Soda Creek, a tributary of Red River, dams which he had located on a scouting trip the day before. At his present camp, he had caught six beaver which he felt was about enough to be taken from one colony of beaver. Had he been trapping in hostile country, he would have moved his camp every day so as to give the hostiles as little chance for ambush as possible.

His beaver sets were only about a quarter of a mile upstream from the camp and it did not take him long to find the "floating stick" and the big male beaver caught by the rear foot in his first underwater set which had been placed at the bottom of a slide. The weight of the five pound trap and a sack of sand attached to the chain had quickly drowned the beaver soon after it had been trapped. Josh took the beaver from the trap and, with a dexterity developed through the performance of the act many times over, quickly stripped from the animal his furry hide. This he shoved along with the trap into his trap sack, picked up the floating stick, and walked across the beaver dam to a second trap set in the underwater entrance to a lodge. There he found the trap sprung but in it were only a few short brown guard hairs. "That hyar one won't make it to St. Louie this y'er," Josh mused to himself. He visited his next three sets and found in one a small kit beaver. He had now caught eight animals from this colony and, picking up his traps, floating sticks, and the carcass of the kit which would make him a good meal, he headed for camp. The mountain man spent little time hunting for food while trapping and subsisted for the most part on beaver and on animals that wandered too close to camp. Even at that, there were some who said that roast beaver tail "throws buffalo boudins in the shade."

Josh spent the remainder of the morning fleshing and graining the skins, scraping as much of the sinew, tissue, and fat as possible from the skin. He then stretched the skins on circular willow hoops to cure and dry for a couple of days before he folded them together for packing.

After Josh had stretched the plew on the willow frame, he ran his hand lightly over the prime rich brown fur and the flow of the hairs from beneath his hand reminded him of the wind blowing across a field of grain. Yet he pondered on the whims of men whose desire for a fashionable hat had prompted and sustained the search for beaver and thereby the age of the mountain man. It was only the bravest of the brave who withstood the rigors of the fierce wilderness to tear from its icy grasp this much sought for prize.

Along about noon, after he had eaten as much of the roasted beaver kit as he could hold, Josh saddled up his stock and traveled west, following game trails, and crossed the divide between Meadow and Soda Creeks. About two miles south of Soda Creek Point, he located a new camp from which he would again set his traps.

Beaver were trapped in the icy waters of the high mountain streams, skinned, stretched, scraped and dried, sewn up into 100 pound packs, and transported to a rendezvous, there to be traded for food, whiskey, guns, traps, and foofaraw, and to be carried by canoe or horseback and keelboat to St. Louis and from there to the eastern seacoast thousands of miles away and there made into felt for hats. It was a mundane end for a beaver that served as the impetus to a vocation that was as glamorous as it was fearsome.

A tangential benefit of the age of the mountain man was the occupation of the territory in which the beaver were indigenous and the ultimate extension of the limits of an emerging nation unwittingly by those who sought an unfettered life and a quick fortune. It was these few adventurous mountain men who were the forerunners of the multitude of settlers which was to follow, who were guided to the west by these same mountain men, and who gained for the nation immense lands that had heretofore been under the influence of the Hudson's Bay Company and the North West Company and whose allegiance was to England.

In contrast to the glamour affixed to the life of a mountain man, this was not a vocation for the faint-hearted and lazy, for the work was cold and exhausting. Good prime beaver were trapped during the time of year when the weather and the water were the coldest and the trapper spent many hours setting and lifting traps in the ice cold water and living with wet feet and clothing. And because of Indian hostiles, only a small smokeless fire with which to warm aching feet and hands could be afforded. Many were the mountain men who developed rheumatism and ague from the long hours of exposure. Small wonder that the trappers took to living with the Indians for the winter or better yet, built themselves cabins during the summer from which they did their trapping during the fall and spring.

Very few of those who partook of the life of the trapper lived to an age so that they could tell their grandchildren about it. Of the hundreds of mountain men who traveled to the Rocky Mountains, only a few ever returned to their homes to relate their adventures.

Trapping was done in a fearsome wilderness, and it grabbed at you with a ferocity that only constant vigilance of its punitive quality permitted a livelihood. Cold, hunger, heat, thirst, and fear are conditions which in their extreme are never appreciated by those who have never experienced them. Cold can be so painful that death is welcomed. Hunger can be so engrossing that man may resort to eating anything, even adopting cannibalism until the insatiable desire is satisfied. Heat can be so exhausting and consuming that man may throw away all protection from the sun and the elements to try to alleviate its oppression. Thirst and its accompanying painful and swollen and cracked tissue can leave a man so dehydrated that he will drink his own bodily excretions in an attempt to satisfy a mind-numbing desire for moisture. Fear, along with its depression, can be so obsessing that it can kill as quickly as can cold or heat. It can derange the mind so thoroughly that the man will drive himself so far beyond human limits that he will often die from exhaustion. The life of a mountain man was so thoroughly permeated with these privations that only self-discipline enabled those who chose the life to survive.

Day after day of wet feet from water that got colder and colder soon takes its toll and the mountain man, in spite of his physical toughness, begins to think of a warm tipi and of food prepared by a woman.

Josh trapped on into late November, traveling to the lower tributaries of the Kooskooski River, forced there by deepening snows and frozen streams. During the last week in November, a snowstorm of monumental proportions, the kind the sow bear looks for to hide the tracks she makes into the den where she will hibernate for the winter, had overnight dropped two feet of powder snow on the country around the Buffalo Hump where his camp was located on Crooked River. Josh took stock of his trapping success and found that he had caught and pelted over one hundred beavers. This was more beaver than he had ever caught previously in both the fall and the spring hunts. It was, he decided, all the beaver he needed to replenish his larder for another year at the annual rendezvous. Also he had been spending a lot of time thinking about the Indian maiden at Stites, and as the ground froze harder and the weather got steadily colder, he thought more and more of a warmer climate in the low country along the Kooskooski River. The storm made up his mind to pull out for a warmer place.

Josh put his pack together, including his hard fought for beaver plews, and riding his Appaloosa stallion and leading his two pack animals, he traveled rapidly westward down the south fork of the Kooskooski. He rode steadily for two days until he came to the vicinity of Lightning Creek which enters the south fork just downstream from where the south fork makes its big turn from flowing west to north, and about twelve more miles up stream from where the south fork and the middle fork join to form the Kooskooski River. Here the ground was bare of snow and frozen only an inch or so below the surface. Here, also, he decided to cache most of his furs, keeping only enough for collateral and trading purposes. He did not want the Nez Perce to know that he had been quite as successful as he had been, and then there was the problem of spending the winter protecting his property while in winter camp. He would retrieve his catch from the cache in the spring just before he made the trip to the rendezvous that would be held in July in Cache Valley along the Bear River in Utah.

As he rode along the trail, Josh searched the sides of the steep hills that ran down to the river for a natural cave under an overhang of basalt, successive layers of which had been exposed by erosion on the sides of the hills. He found just what he had been looking for not far downstream from Three Mile Creek where he saw an opening under an overhand of rock that appeared to satisfy his needs. It was nearing night, so he made camp by the river and when darkness had quenched the fleeting rays of sunset he carried his 100 pound pack of beaver the hundred and fifty yards up the hill and dug a hole under the overhang that was large enough to take the bale of about sixty-six beaver pelts. The furs were sewn tightly in a tanned deer hide bag and were well protected from moisture and insects. After he had dug the hole, he covered the bottom of the cache with boulders so to allow some space for any accumulation of water. On top of the boulders, he laid down a layer of sticks to support the pack, covered it with a well-tanned apishamore, and carefully filled dirt around it. When the cache was completed, he rearranged the vicinity of the cache to appear as near as possible to its original configuration before digging the hole.

Morning came slowly, for a dull gray sky that hung low over the valley permitted little light to filter through. It also brought a steady drizzle of cold rain which further placed the stamp of secrecy on the cache of furs. As he rode away from the cache, Josh noted the landmarks in the vicinity, particularly the peculiar outcroppings of rock, and estimated their distance and direction from the cache. He would want to be able to identify the location of the furs whether it was day or night.

Fourth Interlude
The Beaver

October brings snow to the high country of the Bitterroot Mountains, and the perky red squirrel frantically stores up pine cones for its winter food in secret and often forgotten places. The omnivorous sow black bear has eaten huge quantities of all of the food she can get her paws on or her teeth into. She has consumed huge amounts of huckleberries, elderberries, gooseberries, and snowberries and she quivered as she walked from the thick layer of stored fat and her hair glistened as her muscles moved. Her large soft piles of droppings are full of white snowberry hulls. She is visibly nervous and awaits the great snowstorm that lies just over the horizon that will hide her tracks into her winter's lair. She has mated in the spring and will give birth to two black cubs in February.

The old tom beaver has been busier than usual, cutting down aspen trees, the bark of which serves as his favorite food during the winter. The limbs he will store by sticking their ends into the mud at the bottom of the beaver pond well below the ice that will ultimately cover his world. He and his mate, along with their two half-grown kits that were born during the past spring, will spend the winter within the protection of their well-constructed and almost impervious lodge. This latter edifice is located in the middle of a pond and is about six feet high and twice as wide. The access to the living area is through underwater tunnels. There they will be safe from the wolf, the coyote, and the cougar who would tear apart the almost impregnable frozen mound if given the opportunity and make a meal of the beaver.

The beaver is quite well adapted to the environment in which he lives as he spends most of his life in the water. He has a coat of fur that is essentially waterproof, a set of transparent eyelids which permit underwater vision, nose and ear valves which close underwater, and well-developed webs between the toes on his rear feet. He is a strong swimmer and can tow through the water large logs with which he builds his dams and his houses. With an extra large lung capacity and a large liver for carrying oxygenated blood, he can stay under water as long as fifteen minutes at a time. This ability serves not only to protect him from predators but also is of considerable aid when constructing dams and houses. The beaver is a rodent with very strong teeth and can chew through a five-inch tree in three minutes. It also has the strength to drag the tree to the water where it can be utilized for dam construction or for food.

The dam itself is an engineering marvel. By interweaving sticks, the beaver can build the framework of the dam and yet let water through until it is of sufficient size and strength to create a large volume of water. The beaver then methodically adds to the bottom of the dam face mud and stones and more sticks until he has the dam constructed and the water backed up to adequately protect his home and provide enough depth to serve as a storage for his winter's food supply. The top of the dam face is so interlaced with sticks that the water can spill through without washing them or the sod and dirt away and thus destroy the dam. In case there is a rupture in the dam face brought about by such things as a herd of stampeding buffalo or high water, the beaver will set to work and repair the break by drifting large sticks into the breach and then placing smaller sticks behind the stopper.

The old tom beaver is nearly four feet long from the tip of his black nose on his small-eyed, toothy face to the end of his scaly flat tail. He weighs about sixty pounds and his dense brown fur is prime by winter. Now it has thickened and he is wrapped in a hide, a "plew," that is eagerly sought by the trappers for it is worth six dollars in St. Louis or Montreal.

In spite of the difficulties in trapping and transporting the beaver hide to a far-off land where it will be made into a fashionable felt hat, it was sought for and obtained in quantities that made men rich.

The word beaver was the magic word that thrilled the latent adventurous spirit of every young man on the early nineteenth century frontier of the United States, as would another magic word, gold, some twenty odd years later. There was quick fortune to be made in trapping beaver on the hard-scrabble frontier where a dollar was tough to come by. Just imagine beaver at six dollars a plew, just there for the taking! Why a man could catch a hundred or more in a winter. Waugh! What a life! The search for beaver also embodied a life that was free of all personal restraints in an age when religious and social structures were very rigid. Where in all the land could you get rich and at the same time enjoy the carefree company of other mountain men, to say nothing of the Indian women who would bed down with you for "foofaraw" — a little of nothing — a piece of red ribbon, a handful of blue beads, or a pinch of vermilion? The life held glamour beyond all comprehension. To be able to live a free unfettered life, to fight Indians, and to marry a friendly Indian maiden that you could, if you wished, get rid of by merely shooing her out the door.

It was beaver that was the initial stimulus for the extended exploration of the United States, the Louisiana Territory, the Oregon Country, and the land west of Hudson's Bay in Canada.

It was beaver that in 1673 had led fur trader Louis Joliet and Father Jacques Marquette to the Mississippi River, had led Pierre de La Verendrye in 1738 to Saskatchewan and the Black Hills of South Dakota, had led Simon Fraser, partner of the North West Company of Montreal down the river named for him, the Fraser River in British Columbia where he wintered on the Pacific coast the same year, 1805-06, as had Lewis and Clark wintered at Fort Clatsop at the mouth of the Columbia River in Oregon.

It was beaver that had led Alexander Mackenzie of the North West Company to make the transcontinental trip in 1793 across Canada to the Pacific coast, about which he wrote a book. Thomas Jefferson, president of the United States, read that book and it accelerated his plans to send an American overland expedition to the Pacific coast that came to be led by Captain Meriwether Lewis and Lieutenant William Clark in 1804-06.

Chapter 5
Winterin'

As the days shortened and the cold strengthened, the thoughts of the mountain man turned to finding a tolerable place to live for winterin'. The months of December, January, and February in the high country were fearsome at times. Not only was it often cold enough to freeze and explode a tree, snow was often twenty feet deep. The deep snow drove the mountain man's vital source of food, the deer and the elk, from the high country.

So it was that during the moons of the deep cold, the Indian and the mountain man followed the food supply down to the warmer natural parks in the low valleys along the rivers and streams.

Astride his Appaloosa stallion, Josh rode down the trail along the South Fork of the Kooskooski River, a stream across which you could throw a stone almost anywhere, along which the Nez Perce village was located on a flat flood plain about four miles above the confluence of the South Fork and the Middle Fork which together form the main river.

There was snow spitting from the dark gray clouds which rubbed the tops of the ridges that rose on either side of the river and the wind that whipped the mane of his horse also brought to his nostrils the smell of cooking fires and the fetid odor of habitation. Josh was also aware that his mind was obsessed with the thoughts of Shining Moon. It was good that he was in the country of the friendlies as he was having trouble concentrating on and recognizing the many signals that were being channeled to his brain by his eyes, ears, and nose.

Josh was not so moonstruck, though, that he had forgotten to check the prime in the pan of his rifle and brace of pistols. He had, however, replaced the fringed and decorated elk skin sheath on his rifle as a symbol of peace. He was also aware that for the last hour the signs told him that he was not alone in the wilderness and that unseen eyes were watching his progress down the river valley toward the Nez Perce village. Although he had been proclaimed a brother of the Nez Perce, he was always apprehensive of what the Indian was about and he wore in sight the elk tooth necklace given to him by the chief of the Stites band, Chief Black Elk.

As he rode farther down the valley, Josh observed that the ponderosa pines were more sparsely sprinkled over the very steep brown hills. The now forgotten heat of summer had browned the nutritious bunch grass which covered the foothills on which he could now see many grazing horses.

The wetter draws on the hillsides were overgrown with bushes of the serviceberry, thornberry, and elderberries from which the yellow leaves had long since dropped to the ground. Along the lower slopes were strips of red-leaved sumac bushes. The river was bordered with cottonwood and willow trees now almost completely bare of leaves, only a few of which clung tenaciously to the stark gray limbs and fluttered their last in the cold west wind.

From the border of willows along the near side of the river, his eyes caught a movement of gray and he saw the forms of two deer standing alertly watching his approach, making noses for his scent. Josh stopped his horse, unsheathed his Hawken, and at seventy-five yards dropped the four-point buck mule deer in his tracks with a shot through its neck. He watched the doe as she splashed across the riffle in the river, running away from her dead mate. Josh eviscerated the deer and threw the 'innards' away as he did not wish to salvage them and placed the carcass over the parfleche packs on Midnight's back and continued his journey toward the Nez Perce village.

* * *

The Nez Perce were rich in horses for this was a land of abundant food with a temperate climate which was well protected from the elements as well as from marauding Indians by the surrounding mountains. The Bitterroot Range presented a formidable barrier to the warlike Indians of the plains to the east while the Indians that lived to the west along the Kimnoolnim (Snake) River existed principally on a fish economy and had found little use for horses. The one exception to this was the Cayuse Indians who, like the Nez

Perce, had evolved from a strictly fish economy by supplementing their diet with the products of the buffalo economy.

A strong and intelligent nation, the Nez Perce were not often attacked or raided by neighboring tribes. They were almost self-sufficient in their mountain domain and had little real need to range far from the natural mountain fortress where their forefathers had lived for centuries. However, in recent years, after they had become owners of horses, they had traveled over the mountains to the east in search of the buffalo and to trade with the Flathead, the Crow, and the Shoshone who possessed materials and desirable goods not indigenous to their own homeland.

Linguistically, the Nez Perce spoke the Sahaptin language which was of Penutian stock. The Nez Perce mingled with and were often allies of the Flatheads in a common fight against the Pahkees (Blackfeet) and the Gros Ventres (Atsina). The customs of the Flatheads and the Nez Perce were similar and they often lived together and intermarried. The Flathead Indians spoke the Salishan language and inhabited the eastern slope of the Bitterroot Mountains.

* * *

As the well-worn trail crossed a promontory, forcing it well above the river, Josh rode into full view and beheld before him the thrilling sight of the Nez Perce village composed of a large centrally located reed mat covered lodge which was almost a hundred feet long and around which was scattered approximately twenty leather lodges that constituted the winter camp of the people of Black Elk's band. Josh estimated the band to be about two hundred and seventy-five people strong. The tipis appeared to be identical to those of the plains Indians and had been, he knew, copies from them, while the mat-covered long house was not familiar to him. It was only when the Nez Perce became owners of horses and developed a taste for buffalo meat that they came to need a portable home, the leather tipi. The Indians who existed on a salmon economy lived in the same relative area the year around, as their principal source of food, the anadromous salmon, moved into and up the rivers year after year. The traditional long "pit house" of the Nez Perce that had been used for centuries was a long common house in which as many as one hundred or more people might live. It was constructed of bark and reed mats. The mats were made of cattails and teasel leaves and laid over a framework of wooden poles. The floor of the house was a pit dug down into the ground and the excavated dirt piled up around the perimeter. From this mode of construction came the name given to the edifice — the pit house. These houses were adequate and liveable, albeit not as portable as was the leather tipi.

Adjacent to the pit houses were located the sudatory houses in which the young men and boys of the tribe lived. The wooden frame of these buildings were covered with rye grass on which was piled dirt. Mats made of dried grass covered the dirt floor. The occupants would on occasion pile heated rocks inside their house on which they would throw water. The steam and their sweating cleansed their bodies. The perspiring occupants would then dive into the cold water of the river. They felt these purification baths would counteract any evil which might befall them and were a ritual to be engaged in before departing on a dangerous mission.

Another auxiliary structure to be found in a Nez Perce village was a partially underground lodge for women and adolescent girls. The women stayed in these lodges during their menstrual periods and each girl lived in the lodge at the onset of puberty. These lodges were off limits to men and were also the location of whatever puberty rites were engaged in by the mothers and daughters.

The Nez Perce camp at Stites was well located for protection from the cold east wind, nestled as it was against Battle Ridge which rose up sharply behind the village to the east. The mountains to the south and west fell away up Cottonwood Creek drainage permitting the low winter sun to warm the lodge sites.

As Josh approached the camp, he was greeted by the yapping of scrawny dogs but he detected no other unusual commotion at his approach. He observed that at the edge of the camp near the river were many drying racks on which were hung for curing a few salmon trout — the anadromous rainbow trout, the steelhead. Also hanging on the racks were strips of venison being dried into cherqui (jerky). Extending into the rapids of the river were traps designed to impede the progress of migrating fish up the river, below which the Indians would spear or net fish. This was the time of year when the salmon trout migrated up the Columbia River and its tributaries from the sea, a trip of about four hundred miles. The salmon trout had over the centuries made the easier run up the rivers when the water was low during the fall months of the year, to lie in the deeper holes in the river during the winter awaiting the month of April when they would spawn then to return to the sea with the spring flood, unlike the salmon which died after spawning. The spawned progeny of the steelhead would remain in the rivers until they were a year old and were six to seven inches long and with the spring flood of the following year would travel to the sea where they would spend two to four years feasting on the prolific food supply, grow to an average weight of thirteen pounds, and then migrate up the river of their birth to complete the cycle of regeneration and spawn another generation of fish.

The Nez Perce had subsisted on the anadromous fish for the centuries before they possessed horses, depending on the salmon for a large part of their food supply. It was this continually replenished and repetitive cycle that had attracted the Indians to the rivers of the western slope which afforded them a place with a relatively temperate climate where they could depend on the return of the fish year after year, the "hillal" to provide them with their principal food supply.

In the years before the latter part of the seventeenth century when the Nez Perce first became the owners of horses and before the coming of the white man, the "Long Knives," to their homeland, a supply of fish that were easy to catch with assured availability year after year fostered a way of life that was one of enjoyable existence. In fact, the temperate climate and the encircling geographical features of the Columbia Basin which served as barriers to invasion, along with the abundant food supply, provided for the Nez Perce Indian an enviable standard of living even in a hostile wilderness habitat. Few native tribes existed in such a disease-free, abundant society anywhere in the Western World as did the Nez Perce Indians. It was the coming of the Long Knives with their diseases and the unneeded gift of horses and the availability of trade goods consisting of guns and tools of civilization that changed a society that had for centuries enjoyed an existence as free as man has ever lived, bound only by the parameters of earth and sky.

With the acquisition of the horse, the Nez Perce expanded their horizons and soon developed an appetite for other foods and materials. Even before they became owners of guns, they were riding horseback east of the Bitterroot Mountains along the Nez Perce and Lolo Trails in search of the abundant buffalo and its associated benefits. They came heir to the buffalo hide, hump-ribs, boudins, pemmican, and other seemingly essential items of the buffalo culture. The buffalo came to provide a continuous source of food as had the salmon. Now the diet of the Nez Perce became more varied and nature provided them with myriads of materials which they had not previously known, especially the hide of the buffalo which was made into shelters and clothes — all soon becoming necessary items in the standard of living.

* * *

Josh noted the arrangement of the leather lodges that were positioned in a generally circular pattern around the centrally located common house. Placed near the center of the leather tipis was what appeared to be a double lodge which he recognized to be the residence of the "dog soldiers," men who had been most recently elevated to warrior status and on whom was placed the responsibility of the security of the camp. He also noted a much decorated lance, a totem from which hung many scalps, thrust into the ground in front of the larger leather tipi on the western edge of the center compound of the camp. He recognized the tipi as probably the lodge of Black Elk, chief of the Stites Nez Perce and also the home of Shining Moon.

Approaching closer to the village, Josh watched the smoke curling through the winged vents at the tops of the tipis and from the vent in the top of the long house as it drifted downwind to be whipped and mixed with the spitting snow. It was then that Josh became aware of the movement from beyond the willows near the river, along the west side of the camp, of a procession of riders circling to the eastward behind him. The movement was gradual and without urgency and although Josh was curious as to the reason for the assemblage, he was not particularly apprehensive, for the participants were without paint and regalia and showed no sign of hostility. He continued his progress toward the village showing no indication of fear or concern. It was then that he recognized Black Elk moving toward him from the assembled group holding up his hand in sign of peace. Josh was, within himself, somewhat relieved even though he had made no outward sign of fear. He stopped his animals and awaited the approach of the chief. Black Elk made signs welcoming Josh to the village and motioned for Josh to follow him to the village, to be royally welcomed with food, drink, and praise because of his service to the family of the chief. His presence in the vicinity and approach to the village had been known for some time as the Nez Perce had monitored his progress down the trail and had awaited him to make the show of welcome. Many people now came out of their lodges and approached the huge mountain man who had been the topic of conversation around the council fires for these past three moons. They were curious and wished to shake the hand and touch this brave Long Knife who had singlehandedly rescued Shining Moon, the daughter of their chief, from the Pahkee war party.

It was then that Josh saw standing before the chief's lodge the maiden whom he had come, for the past three months, to think and dream about so often. Word that the huge mountain man was approaching the Nez Perce village had reached the ears of Shining Moon some time before he rode into sight down the river from the east. During the past three moons, her thoughts, too, had often reflected back to her capture by the Pahkees and to her welcomed rescue by the Long Knife. He, who against considerable odds, had engaged in and defeated in hand to hand combat her six Pahkee captors.

Shining Moon was at the age when most Nez Perce women were taken in marriage and she was a prize sought for by many warriors of her own and neighboring tribes. She was the beautiful daughter of a rich war chief and could have taken her pick of almost any Indian brave she wished. She was four years past puberty, was lithe and slim, and desireable. She could be expected to select a husband at any time. She had, however, spurned all offers of marriage by her suitors. Within the past moon, she had been hard pressed by Ilp Ilp Waptas, Red Eagle, to be his wife. Red Eagle was the son of Neesh-Ne-Pah-Keook, Cut Nose, whose name had come from his nose having been cut by a lance in a battle with the Snake Indians and who was chief of the tribe residing at the confluence of the Potlatch River with the Kooskooski. But Shining Moon had declined his offer of many horses. Had her father been poor in horses, there would probably not have been any choice in the matter. But he, too, was a rich man, the owner of hundreds of horses and because of this wealth, he listened to the wishes of Shining Moon in the matter of marriage.

It was the custom among the Nez Perce that when a warrior wished to marry an Indian maiden, he would place outside her lodge the dowry of horses and other gifts he desired to trade to the father in exchange for his daughter. If the daughter were amenable to the marriage and the father thought the dowry was of sufficient amount, the horses would be placed with his herd and the other material taken into the lodge and the marriage would be consumated. If, however, the marriage was not acceptable to the maiden or the amount of the dowry was considered insufficient, the dowry would be left where it had been placed, in which case the unfortunate suitor would retrieve his offering and return to his home without a wife.

It was also because of the wealth of her father that Shining Moon had not been offered to any visitors as was often the case with many young Indian women. It was not unusual for a father or a husband to sell the pleasures of his daughter or even his wife to the mountain men or traders for a drink of whiskey or a rifle. Sex to an Indian was commonplace and attached were no inhibitions or stigma. The Indian maiden was pleased with any bit of foofaraw for her attention, when an Indian buck could extract the same from her in the bushes for nothing.

In fact, the Indian could not understand the attitude and constant desire for the attention of Indian women by the Long Knives. They wondered whether the white man had white women at home, as they had never seen any white women in the company of the mountain men. It was usual for the Indian women to travel with their men almost everywhere they went, except on a war party, and it was a mystery to the Indian why white women did not accompany the mountain men.

To the Indian, sex was a common everyday affair and invoked little discussion. Sex was to the Indian brave to be taken whenever and wherever he desired.

To the mountain man, the attitude of the Indian toward sex was a revelation, for he had been reared in a society which placed a penalty on sexual promiscuity and his resultant sex desire for a time became insatiable. When only a small piece of cloth, a few beads, or a small sack of vermilion was the price of a woman, it turned a rendezvous or wintering with the Indians into a delight of unlimited love-making. In the society of most Indian tribes, about the only penalty for promiscuity was that of contracting the Rocky Mountain Quick Step — gonorrhea, but that was just one of the hazards and did not deter the mountain man from pursuing his favorite pastime of satisfying the solace of his body. But then, who is to evaluate on the basis of their own society the morals and mores of another society as has been the practice of the so-called "superior white society." The Indian sought just as avidly elements of the white man's society. They would seek to learn more of his religion — his Medicine — because it provided the white man with greater possessions than had the Indian. He sought religion, not because it answered the unanswered questions of an after-life, but because of the existing life.

* * *

Shining Moon had spent her spare moments these past three months, when not engaged in helping her mother with the continuous drudgery of daily living, in making clothing which she thought would be becoming to her. She had on many occasions during the time wondered if the huge mountain man would travel to her village for the winter as he had told her father, Black Elk, that he would.

She had made a new winter garment for herself from the skin of a bighorn sheep, the sewing of which she had spent many hours. First tanning the hide until it was almost white, then continually scraping until it was very thin, and then rubbing the fine soft leather with the white clay which had been dug in the clay beds sixty miles to the northwest at the headwaters of the Potlatch River. She had decorated the garment with porcupine quills which had been dyed in many colors from dyes that were made from the juices of berries and from the boiling of mosses and lichens. For decoration, she had also used the quills of birds, small bones and teeth from small animals and particularly the bones of the Raven which was her own personal Wyakin. These decorations were sewn to the garment in attractive patterns with split sinew taken from the back of the buffalo.

Shining Moon had also sewn winter moccasins which were made from the year-old tipi cover which after a year of cooking fire smoke was so well cured that articles of clothing made from the leather were almost waterproof and would dry soft when wetted.

Shining Moon had also made an extra fringed shirt and pair of trousers of soft elk skin, larger than she had ever made before. At the time of her rescue from the Pahkees by the mountain man, she had noticed how large he was and that the clothes that he wore were showing the worse for wear. Indian clothing was made without the benefit of a pattern and the Indian women became proficient in the sewing of clothing from memory, albeit ill-fitting at times. Each Indian mother passed on to her daughters the expertise to do many of the necessary chores of survival, one of which was the ability to make clothing from materials gleaned from nature. Shining Moon had also made some fur-lined winter moccasins from the winter buffalo hide tanned with the hair on. Knee-length leggings lined with snowshoe hare fur were sewn to the top of the moccasins. These leggings were warm and served well while horseback riding in the winter. In spite of the limited supply and availability of materials for sewing, a small sharp bone for an awl, the split sinew from the back of the buffalo for thread, the hides of animals, the long hours of work which must go into the tanning of hides, the Indian even before the advent of trade goods from the Long Knives was adequately dressed to subsist even in the coldest weather. The Indian was often referred to by the mountain man as being all face, as he wore a minimum of clothing, even in the coldest weather.

* * *

As Josh cast his eyes on the lithe and enticing form of Shining Moon as she stood before her buffalo skin lodge, all of his thoughts of the past three months came rushing back to him like a spring flood. The mental image of her beauty that had pervaded his mind was real and had not been imagined. All through these long cold winter evenings when his thoughts had been consumed not only with visions of fat buffalo cow, streams full of beaver, he found himself thinking more and more of the warm soft body of this lovely Indian maiden. During those long hours when he had been busy scraping, dressing, and stretching beaver skins and caring for camp and trapping duties, he had turned over in his mind again and again how he was going to convince Chief Black Elk that he, Josh Copeland, would make a proper husband for his daughter.

Josh had spent hours meticulously preparing the speech he would make to his future father-in-law, telling him that when the chief was old and with failing eyes from years of sitting around council fires in smoky tipis, when he could no longer see the seven stars in the Seven Sisters, the Pleiades, and could no longer ride to hunt the buffalo and provide meat for the pot, that he, Josh Copeland, would fetch to camp the deer, the antelope, the mountain sheep, the buffalo, the elk, and the bear for food, for clothing, and for weapons. He would tell the venerable old chief that he, Josh, was a great hunter and a good provider and could shoot plum center with old Bull Shooter, one of Jed Hawken's best rifles.

Josh wanted to convince Chief Black Elk that he would father strong and savvy warriors that would continue the lineage of great Nez Perce chiefs. That he could do more for the chief than could any Nez Perce warrior. In his daydreams, Josh had also often wondered how many young warriors from her own or neighboring tribes, who surely must have noticed the uncommon beauty of this wilderness maiden, had sought her hand in marriage. She was, he well knew, at the age when the young Nez Perce women were being courted.

Josh only hoped that Chief Black Elk had refused all offers for his daughter's hand. But then, how were they, either Shining Moon or the chief, to know that he was intent on matrimony? There had not been any time in the few short hours after her rescue and when they had been together, that he had made any overtures which could have been construed as an indication that he was interested in taking this tawny beauty for his wife.

Josh had, however, decided long before he started down the trail toward the Nez Perce winter camp, that he would offer Chief Black Elk thirty beaver plews for the hand of his daughter. With that number of pelts, Black Elk could trade for guns, powder, and balls with the King George men of the Hudson's Bay Company at Spokane House, which was the nearest British trading post, five days to the north. Or, if he so desired, he could trade the pelts for whiskey, glittering beads, three point blankets, red strouding cloth, or even such mundane things as cooking pots.

If Shining Moon was amenable to accepting him as a husband, Josh rationalized that he could provide her with treasures beyond her fondest dreams. As a considerably better than average free trapper, Josh regularly took beaver enough to buy her vermilion, blue beads, hawk bells, mirrors, and the foofaraw to make any wilderness beauty happy. The wife of a free trapper could surely live in "shinin' times."

The benefits were not, however, all in Shining Moon's favor, for the husband of this Nez Perce maid would also benefit from a marriage. Not only from the solace of the body and the comforting nearness of a partner in the lonesomeness of the wilderness, but his wife had been well schooled by her mother,

Spotted Fawn, in the art of survival in this hostile environment. Shining Moon could dress pelts of the beaver, otter, and muskrat for trading, tan the hides of buffalo, elk, and deer and make from them moccasins, fringed shirts, and breeches. She would skin, butcher, and dry the meat, prepare and cook food that would be very palatable in spite of the limited cooking utensils. She could make and repair a tipi which would serve as a very comfortable shelter; she would strike and raise the tipi before and after travel; she would catch and saddle not only her own and her husband's horses, but also catch and load the pack animals and prepare them for travel. In fact, she would make wilderness living almost bearable, for the good Indian wife left no work for her husband to do.

In the society of the Indian, the husband of a squaw owned his wife completely. He could beat and abuse her as he saw fit and could even kill her without fear of punitive repercussion. In spite of the accepted slavery, the squaw was not without influence in her own household and in the tribe. Although she was not allowed in the council meetings, she did, through her husband, influence the decisions of the governance of the tribe.

The Indian woman could, as well as could the man, leave her husband for another man, and the new husband need only pay the former husband for her value. On occasions, a lecherous old chief who wanted the beautiful wife of a man of lesser rank, would work through an intermediary to gain the woman as a mate. In such cases, the original husband could seek redress through the tribal council. Their decision, however, was final and was usually in favor of the chief.

Custom also gave an unmarried girl the right to disagree with what to her was an undesirable husband and when she disagreed with her father he was required to return to her suitor any price he had accepted for her.

The winning of the hand of Shining Moon proved to be easier than Josh had anticipated. Black Elk, wily old chief that he was, of course, appeared to be reluctant to part with his daughter, and in sign language told of the many great warriors who had come laden with gifts in exchange for her hand, but through it all he had steadfastly refused their offers of many horses. He had made big Medicine, had sought the guidance of the great spirit and his own personal Wyakin, and had smoked many pipes hoping that when the Long Knife who had saved his daughter from slavery among the Pahkees, came to his village to spend the winter as he had promised, that he would consider his daughter for his wife.

Josh explained to Chief Black Elk in sign language that he had thirty beaver pelts to trade for the hand of Shining Moon and that these pelts could in turn be traded for much desirable trade goods. He knew how the Nez Perce felt about trapping for fur, for they looked upon trapping as the work for squaws. However, it was not degrading for Chief Black Elk to trade these fine prime pelts, which Josh had spent many hours catching and dressing, for much useful trade goods. The equivalent value of the pelts was probably about ten horses.

Through the negotiations, Shining Moon stood quietly nearby watching the tempo of the sign language and when asked by her father, "Did she accept this Long Knife as her husband?" she replied that "If he ordered her to the bed of the mountain man, she would obey." But there was no doubt that she approved of the arrangement, for in her face could be seen the beauty of the spring, and in her sparkling dark eyes, the joy of a small child.

Now that the marriage had been arranged and Josh and Shining Moon had stood together under the white elk robe and had received the marriage rites, Josh took this occasion to show his elation and took out of the soft leather case his flute and proceeded to play. It didn't take long for the whole population of the village to surround him and listen enthralled to the rich melodic sounds of Mozart's Concerto in G Major that flowed from the strange-looking stick with holes in it. While the Indian had very few musical instruments, they did have a natural feeling for rhythm and danced to the sounds of the tom-tom, the rattles, and a primitive flute. The tom-tom was made of a piece of rawhide stretched over a hollowed out tree and was their principal musical instrument which provided the cadence to which the Indians danced. The flute was made from two pieces of wood, one hollowed out with the second piece sliding inside the other. The hollow piece had in it at the upper end six holes and was sounded by a reeded mouthpiece. The instrument produced a variable whistling sound but did not match the resonant music of Josh's flute.

They also made rattles from dry gourds which they obtained in trade from more sedentary Indians. Rattles were made from an inch or so of the hoof of the mountain sheep or of a buffalo, a number of which when tied together and attached to a stick and shaken made a rattling sound.

It didn't take Josh long to settle into the routine of winter camp and with his new wife he spent many hours in the tipi provided him by the family of Shining Moon, trying to catch up on what he had been fretting about these past three months.

The life of the Indian men in the winter camp was one of relative ease. With the plentiful supply of food and a warm shelter, the winter was the time of year when stories of past wars and of hunting exploits were recounted over and over. There was also time for making plans for future wars and hunts. The Indian told stories of many things, but his stories were usually of raids and war on other Indians intermixed with stories of animals and the Indian's close association to them. The Indian mind was never burdened with the difference between the man and the animal and his stories treated each as equals as characters in a tale.

Without the need to search daily for food, the Indian spent many hours at story telling, at dancing, and traveling up and down the river visiting the neighboring tribes. Winter was also the time for the man to manufacture his hunting tools and war implements. The laminated bow made by the Nez Perce was one sought by many other Indians and not only served the Nez Perce as a hunting and fighting weapon but also was a highly sought after intertribal trade item. The Nez Perce bow was from a section of the horn of the mountain sheep. The horn was straightened by the patient process of steaming, forming, and stretching. The straightened and formed horn was then laminated, backed, and wrapped with deer sinew attached with glue made from the skin of a salmon or sturgeon. When completed and strung with a string made of animal sinew, the three-foot long bow would cast an arrow that would pass through the body of a deer or antelope when shot at close range. When used as a weapon of war, the stone arrowhead was often dipped in poison made from rattlesnake venom. Arrowheads, as a rule, were made of stone chipped out laboriously from flint rock, a rock of conchoidal fracture, and formed by pressing on the edges of the point with a sharp piece of deer or elk horn and by spalling off pieces of the rock until the desired arrowhead shape was achieved. Arrowheads were made in many sizes and selected according to the size of the animal or bird the Indian wished to hunt.

Arrows were made of straight pieces of serviceberry wood, often straightened and sized by forcing the arrow shaft through a hole ground into two abutting sandstone rocks that were held together by sinew or rawhide. The arrow might then be heated and hardened. The feathers were fletched on the rear of the arrow with salmon skin glue and tied with sinew. The bow string was made of animal sinew. The Indian could shoot faster than a man could load and fire a muzzle-loading rifle. The time between shots was often only about five seconds. While the effective range with a bow and arrow was only about 40 to 50 yards, the Indian could shoot an arrow as far as 100 yards without difficulty.

For hunting game, the Indian used the bow and arrow almost exclusively. Even after he became the owner of a gun, he still used the bow and arrow for hunting. He used his gun principally for war because the noise of the gun scared the animals and also revealed his location to others. The bow and arrow was almost silent and at close range the Indian was almost as effective with the bow as he was with the muzzle loading trade gun.

With the gun which had been procured from the British as a weapon of war, the Blackfoot Indians had ruled the territory east of the Rocky Mountains before the Indians west of the Bitterroot Range had procured guns by trade. In fact, the Blackfeet made every effort to prevent the Indians of the Rockies from obtaining guns from the traders and managed to do so for several years.

At the time of Lewis and Clarks' passage through the country of the Nez Perce in 1805-06, the latter owned only a few, probably six, guns all of which had been acquired just a year before (circa 1805) in trade from the Hidatsa Indians who lived along the middle Missouri River.

The Nez Perce desired guns for defense against the Blackfeet who were pressuring them very hard in their travels east of the Bitterroot Mountains to the buffalo country. It is not known for sure when the Blackfeet first acquired guns but when their allies, the Gros Ventres, were first contacted by a Hudson's Bay Company employee by the name of Anthony Henday in the year 1754 they had guns in their possession. This would have been almost fifty years before the Nez Perce acquired guns.

* * *

It would seem that the marriage of two people, each a product of such diverse cultures, would have little chance for success, what with different moral standards, languages, health habits, diets, social structures, traditions, and religions. However, there was a common denominator that each possessed regardless of the cultural differences, and that was the physical attraction that a woman has for a man, and a man for a woman. The lack of a common background and culture does not inhibit the intimacy between a man and a woman. Josh and Shining Moon had developed a love for one another almost from the moment he had looked into the velvet depths of her eyes. Although eons apart in cultural development as measured by the white man's measuring stick, the same emotional feelings exist in a man and a woman at any stage of cultural development.

So it was with Josh and Shining Moon as they took up residence together in a leather tipi in the wilderness village near present-day Stites. From the first, each began learning the traits of the other. While the woman in the Indian society is traditionally the more submissive of the two sexes, they are not, however, lacking in their own rights. As the daughter of a chief of the Nez Perce nation, a princess, Shining Moon had come to exhibit personality traits which might not have evolved had she been the daughter of a lesser warrior of the tribe. She was intelligent and had learned her lessons of survival well, as taught by her mother, Spotted Fawn.

Spotted Fawn herself held a position in the family of Chief Black Elk seldom enjoyed by the wife of any chief. She held sway in many of the decisions of the family and was often sought out as a confidant of Chief Black Elk when making decisions of moment for the tribe.

In the days before Josh had ridden his Appaloosa stallion into the village, Spotted Fawn had been aware of the feeling that her daughter held toward the mountain man. Both Shining Moon and Black Elk had apprised her of the attributes of this man who had saved their daughter from the Pahkees. She still, however, retained her reservations concerning this man until she herself could assess the suitability of a white man as a husband for her daughter. She had watched the advances of Red Eagle, son of the great war chief Cut Nose of the Potlatch River Nez Perce, who had been spurned by her daughter and she withheld her approval of the mountain man until she could form her own opinion of his suitability as a son-in-law.

It was some time after Josh had ridden into the village that Spotted Fawn had taken stock of this mountain man and had given her blessing to the marriage of her daughter to him. Her mind was made up by the look on his face when he gazed on Shining Moon, which so clearly showed the love he had for her daughter.

During the weeks that followed the day when the two lovers stood together beneath the white elk robe that was symbolic of a union of mutual trust, there was exhibited a genuine love of a man for a woman and a woman for a man.

Josh spent many hours learning the customs and traditions of the Nez Perce from his newly-married wife. Here was an Indian princess whose emotions were as free as the birds in the sky, a woman uninhibited and unfettered by a moral code that was imposed on a woman of the so-called civilized world by her peers, little wonder that the mountain man turned to this Indian woman for solace of the body.

Josh marveled at the personality of his wife, for as he came to know her more intimately, he developed a knowing awareness of the people in the society of which he had become a member. She was a creature of the wilderness as free as the young red-tailed hawk riding for the first time to a previously unattainable height on the thermals into the sky.

Shining Moon had grown up in a society unfettered by the bond which he himself had been tied to in his own regimented society. He learned that the Indian placed few limitations on himself for he lived as did the other creatures of the wilderness, irresolute and timid at times and fearless and violent at others, knowing that to stray far from an anomalous path often meant a quick and violent death. There was little need for the group, the tribe, to impose minimal penalties on the individual for minor infractions, for it was permissible for one to kill others who might encroach on your being without any penalty from the group.

Josh watched his wife as she raced her horse with abandon across the limitless prairies of grass uncontained by the fences civilized man imposed on his own existence. She was an agnostic, but yet spiritually attuned to the realities of nature as no civilized man could ever be. She acknowledged no formal superior being, yet recognized her own human limitations, entreating of her companions, the wilderness, her own guardian spirit, help in coping with the unanswerable ordeals and privations she knew she must surmount. The Indian considered that he, his fellow man, and the creatures of the wilderness were equals, for without them he would not long survive.

Josh sat by the campfire by the hour and talked with Shining Moon, first in sign language and later as time passed in Sahaptin, the Nez Perce tongue. He talked with Black Elk and Spotted Fawn about the culture of these people whom he had adopted as they had adopted him.

Shining Moon proved to be a delightful wife for she was always doing things for her husband that she knew would please him. She made him clothing from the softest leathers, underclothing made to wear next to his body from the thinly scraped and tanned skin of the antelope, so soft and pliable that the wearer was almost unaware that he had it on.

The moccasins she made for winter wear were lined with the fur of the snowshoe hare and which kept Josh's feet warm as he rode on the horseback trips they took throughout the domain of the Nez Perce.

Shining Moon showed Josh all of the wonders of her country, particularly the places which were part of the traditions and history of the Nez Perce. One of the sacred places which was located near the village of Chief Broken Arm at Kamiah was the Heart of the Monster, a basalt rock mound which Nez Perce lore said was the heart of the monster which had been slain by Coyote. The Indian legend said that the parts of the slain monster constituted the origin of all Indian peoples and the blood that was sprinkled from the paw of Coyote was the origin of the Chopunnish. The Indian in his wisdom did not differentiate between animal and man. All were brothers in his eyes and they lived together in harmony each with his rightful place in society.

The activities of the Indian were not all drudgery and Josh and Shining Moon spent many days riding through the countryside. Shining Moon attempted to relate to her husband the best things in her life, including the traditions of the tribe which had been passed down from generation to generation by word of mouth through the aspen smoke of history.

Josh was delighted at the affection exhibited by his wife in their intimate sexual encounters, for she would seek the embrace of their bodies with abandon — contact that would leave Josh exhausted by her insatiable desire for his attention. Not that Josh considered this attention undesirable for he was in the prime of his life and he, too, sought the daily attention of his wife, for the feeling of a man for a woman is exhibited in the physical as well as the emotional encounters and so it was with these two lovers.

Josh reflected back in his mind to his life as a young boy and to the lack of intimacy displayed by his parents. He recalled the members of his family had displayed little emotion. His parents had been reasonably stable people who treated each other with respect, were very religious, feared the Lord, and abided by the Ten Commandments.

The life of a family in the hardscrabble world of the eastern Ohio frontier was by any measure both physically and mentally difficult. It was a life that demanded the ultimate in dedication to scratch out an existence and to achieve any set goals. How different was his existence here in this totally different culture which he now so enjoyed, free to do almost as he wished without restriction of any kind.

* * *

And so through the months of December, January, and February, Josh and Shining Moon shared the common bond of love and affection. Josh was accepted into the tribe as a confidant, as an advisor of Chief Black Elk. He was on occasion invited by the chief to sit at the meetings of the tribal council. It did not take the elders of the tribe, these native sons of the wilderness, long to sense the wisdom of this mountain man and they sought his council in their meditation.

It was at one such council meeting that Chief Black Elk entreated the help of the mountain man in gaining for his tribe the religion, the medicine, which gives to the white man all of the material wealth he enjoys.

SPEECH BY BLACK ELK

Oh Long Knife, brother of the Chopunnish, it is true we have lived along the Kooskooski River for many seasons. In the beginning, it was Coyote who killed the monster at Kamiah and from its parts were created all of the people in the land. From the dops of blood on his paws were created the Chopunnish.

The ways of the Chopunnish are like that of no other people for we have no bounds but the earth and the sky and because of this our life has been good. We have much food and good shelter, our children and old people are cared for without want. There are natso'x, the salmon in the rivers; wawu'xya, the elk; ima'snim, the deer; and xaxasnim, the bear, in the mountains. With the melting of the snow, there are kouse roots on the sunny hillsides and camas roots in the meadows in the moon of the longest days.

We have followed in war the great war chief Tunnachemootoolt, Broken Arm, from Kamiah. We have prevailed over our enemies in the days gone by and they seldom tried to count coup in our land. The Bitterroot Mountains to the rising sun have protected us from the war-like Pahkees. We live in peace with our neighbors. The Cayuse, in the highlands and along the rivers to the setting sun and the Coeur d'Alenes and the Kutenais to the star that does not travel are not warlike and with them, too, we live in peace. In the country where the Kimnoolnim River turns to the rising sun, the Teewalka, the Western Shoshone is the enemy to be fought. There is now a truce with the Teewalka that was made this past summer on the Burnt River where it forks with the Kimnoolnim and where we gave our word in peace. The word of the Chopunnish leaders is taken as straight and with concern at the council fires from the big portage rapids (the Dalles) to the setting sun on the great river to the sea (the Columbia), to the great lakes (Pend Oreille and Coeur d'Alene) to the standing star, to the river of the salmon, the Natso'x.

In trade, we have traveled trails to the rising sun and toward the great hunter in the sky and to the great bear who lives by the standing star. In the days of my fathers, came the white horse from the land of the Shoshone in trade to the people at Alpowa Creek. From this pregnant white mare has come the many horses among which are the spotted horses known as the Appaloosa, one of which you are now the owner. These horses are sought by many people for the sure-footedness on the mountain trails.

We have traded with the Long Knives, the King George man, at the trading posts in our land, for the medicine iron. We have not trapped the beaver, the taxtspolya'ya, for trade as they would have us do, but have traded to them the spotted horses. It is those people who are poor in horses and have no horses for trade who trap the beaver. To trap the beaver would require a change in our whole pattern of life. It is because the Long Knives have traded the medicine iron to our enemies that we are now forced to trade our horses. Our bows made fron the horn of the mountain sheep are the best in the land and are even sought by the buffalo hunting people in the land of the rising sun beyond the mountains. It is only for war do we need the trade goods, the medicine iron, the powder and ball of the Long Knives.

We of the Chopunnish have a need for the great medicine that is the religion of the Long Knives for with it we can regain our superior position in the eyes of the people who have for many snows listened to the council of the Chopunnish. It is from the Iroquois, the slaves of the King George men of the North West Company, who have enslaved them with whiskey, that we hear of the medicine of the religion of the Long Knives.

My people and all of the Chopunnish speak at the council fires of your religion and great medicine that comes from it. The medicine iron and the trade goods will give us the power once again to lead my people is what we would seek. We wish to walk again unchallenged in this land, as there are now those who would challenge us for our land, our horses, and our women. You have seen how the Pahkees, the Blackfeet, have tried and would have succeeded in taking my first-born daughter, Shining Moon, from us, had you not stood strong without fear before many warriors.

Oh, Long Knife, give us your council and help us in our search for the great religion that would again give us the power of our forefathers.

*   *   *

And so it was that Josh agreed to talk to the men who traveled with the supply trains that came yearly to the rendezvous about the wishes of the Nez Perces. First, he wished to travel to one of the trading posts in the area to trade for some powder and ball for his guns and some supplies peculiar to the needs of the white man such as salt, sugar, coffee, and tea. The Indian could get along without these supplies, but Josh had not lost all of his civilization habits and liked to have, on occasion, a cup of coffee or tea. He and Shining Moon would leave the village at Stites to make the trip north to the trading posts and from there cross the mountains to the east by way of the water-level route up the Clark Fork River and from there south to the rendezvous in Cache Valley in southern Idaho. He would take with him all the paraphenalia he owned, including his traps, for he would trap the streams along the way and trade the newly caught furs for the supplies he needed. It would be a change from the days of traveling alone, for with his bride of five months he could concentrate on his trapping and hunting and leave the camp chores to Shining Moon. With all this time for trapping, he should have enough pelts to trade for his supplies in no time at all.

Fifth Interlude
The Tipi

The tipi utilized by the Indian was a relatively warm shelter. It was made of several buffalo hides sewn together with animal sinew into a conical shape. The size of the tipi depended on the number of people in the family and the ability of the family to transport it from camp to camp. An average tipi weighed about 200 pounds and was fifteen feet in height with a diameter at the base of about fifteen feet. Some of the larger tipis were as much as eighteen feet in diameter and as tall.

The entrance opening was about five feet in height, over which a buffalo robe hung loosely except in bad weather when it was pulled taut with thongs attached to the lower corners.

To erect the tipi, the conical leather covering was spread flat on the ground and the two overlapping vertical edges fastened together with wooden pegs. Four lodge poles, loosely tied together near the upper end, were thrust under the covering and into the opening at the center of the cover. These poles were then raised by two women standing outside the tipi and pulling on a rawhide rope attached to the top of the poles. A third woman on the inside of the tipi would spread the poles equally around the perimeter of the base of the structure. Other poles were then placed into the crossing of the original poles and forced as tightly as possible against the cover.

Wooden pins were then driven through slits at the bottom of the covering so to make the shelter as air tight as possible. During the winter, snow was packed around the bottom of the covering to further make the shelter airtight for increased comfort.

At the top of the tipi was a leather winged cap that was adjusted by poles which were fastened with rawhide thongs to the cap and could be arranged so as to direct the smoke and air. The opening was adjusted to face downwind which utilized the negative pressure created by the wind to draw the smoke from inside the tipi. Obviously, this arrangement was only partially successful as the wind direction in a desirable sheltered location was variable. But the arrangement was adequate, albeit smoky and eye-smarting, for the occupants. However, it was possibly a major cause of the large amount of eye trouble, the trachoma, reported by Lewis and Clark, that was prevalant among the Nez Perce.

Leather curtains three or four feet high were often sewn into the lower edges of the tipi, providing a dead air space and yet greater comfort for the occupants. Tanned animal skins were placed on the ground for rugs and with a fire located in the center, the tipi was a relatively warm home, even in the coldest weather and with the use of very little fuel.

Beds were made of a pile of buffalo hides taken during the winter, tanned with the hair on, and positioned around the perimeter as near to the curtains and cover as possible. There was also a pillow made from the hide of a small animal such as a coyote or a badger and stuffed with grass. Other furniture included back rests made of a v-shaped frame and rawhide thongs. These were also used as protection between the person and the direct heat of the fire.

Over the centrally located fire, there usually hung a kettle in which food was cooked. The Indian observed no regular eating hours and as a rule ate only one meal a day, which he took from the common pot with his fingers or his knife.

The location of the lodge within the village was often a matter of the occupants' status within the tribe, with the lodges of the chief and principal men located in the center of the village and the people of lesser rank located without regard to order outside this circle. The followers of a particular chief or principal man might locate their tipis in close proximity to the rear of the tipi of that man.

The enclosed circle at the center of the village was used for war and ceremonial dances, for bragging and strutting, and for gambling and trading. The location of the winter camp was important and involved much discussion in council. The Nez Perce were not as nomadic as were the plains Indians and returned year after year to the same relative location for their winter camp. In fact, some people might stay at a river camp the year around. The availability of food, water, and wood for fire, and grass for the ponies was of primary consideration in the location of the winter camp.

For the tribe at peace, winter camp was an enjoyable time of the year. The warriors spent much of the day gambling and reserved the evenings for the telling of stories. For the young of both sexes, it was a time of unending excitement and pleasure. There were feasts and dances with interfamily and intertribal visitation with much love-making. In fact, love ruled the camp. During the evening, the beat of the tom-tom was the signal for a dance which might last all night. Such dances were usually held in the large lodges near the center of the village.

Even the old people and the women enjoyed the winter camp for there was no work to be done in erecting and striking of the tipis, no long days of travel, and no packing and unpacking of duffle, and only a minimal amount of heavy work.

The warrior of means often spent much of the day gambling and the evening at story telling. His gambling usually consisted of participating in a "game of hand" in which four players usually engaged. But there are always lots of betters surrounding the game. The game is performed by one of the players holding in his hand a piece of bone, well polished from frequent use. The piece of bone is usually long and thin, about two or three inches in length, and half an inch or so in diameter. The purpose of the game is to identify which hand the bone is held in. The players are divided into two teams with two players on a team. One of the players holds the bone in his hand, switching it back and forth with considerable dexterity between the hands, permitting occasional glimpses of the bone when the hands are touching so as to give the illusion that the bone is in one hand but usually ends up in the other. The other three players watch closely and eventually one of the players on the opposing team feels confident enough to make a selection and points to one of the hands, which is immediately opened. If the bone was in the selected hand, that side or team is credited with a point. If the bone is not in the hand selected, then the other team wins the point. When one side gains twenty-one points, that team wins and may collect on the bets which have previously been made. The game is then resumed when bets have again been made by the players as well as those who were watching.

The game is enjoyed by many Indians even though two

players usually make up a team. Bets are made and each player tries to match each bet with something more valuable than that bet by opposing players. It is at this point in the game when there is considerable noise as a result of the bargaining and wrangling. But once the bets are made and the "making of the game" satisfied, the game proceeds. At the end of the game, there is no controversy as the bets have already been laid and the fortunate players gather up their winnings. As in all games of chance, the participants may start the game with considerable wealth and end up a pauper. So it is with the Indian who might become so desperate that after losing all his meager worldly goods he might wager his wife in an attempt to recoup his losses. To add to the tempo of the game the tom-tom is often kept beating throughout the play and a game may last for hours.

Winter camp is also a time when there is lots of dancing night after night. The Indian woman is as vain as a peacock and will in the evening dress herself in her best finery and stand outside of her lodge awaiting the sound of the tom-tom that signals to all in the village the beginning of a dance. It is then, that many in the tribe would congregate in either one large tipi or in a special tipi made from two which have been moved close together. Social dances are ruled by the women and involve individuals dancing either by themselves or if so motivated, a woman might select a warrior from the audience to dance with. They could dance either arm in arm or by facing each other with their arms around each other, their moccasined feet scuffing the dirt in short steps with the weight of the body on the ball of the foot, their heels not touching the ground. The shoulders rising and falling with nervous motions of the body, all to the tempo of the tom-tom.

Chapter 6
Spring Travels

With the advent of spring weather, there is much activity in the Nez Perce village. Preparations are being made by members of the tribe for excursions to many different places. There is still vast accumulations of snow in the high country of the Bitterroot Mountains to the east and the Salmon River Mountains to the south that will preclude travel over these mountains until the month of June. It is possible during the months of March and April to follow the lowland water courses to the west down the Kooskooski to the Kimnoolnim and to the Columbia River. Intertribal trade with the Pacific Coast and lower river Indians had been carried on for centuries at The Dalles, a portage where travel up and down the Columbia River was interrupted by a series of cataracts. More recently, a trading post, "Fort Nez Perces" had been built about one-half mile above the confluence of the Walla Walla River with the Columbia just upriver from where the Columbia makes the big turn from south to west toward the Pacific Ocean. The trading post was erected by the North West Company of Montreal for trading with the Nez Perce, Walla Walla, Cayuse, Yakima, Palouse, and other river Indians. It was built in 1818 under the direction of Donald "Perpetual Motion" McKenzie of Astor's Pacific Fur Company fame. He, along with 95 men, Canadians, Iroquois, and Owyhees built the fort, which soon came to be known as the Gibraltar of the Columbia! The fort was about 100 feet square and constructed of stone houses and ramparts, with a firing gallery, bastions, swivel guns, cannons, and a main gate of iron. It was a veritable impregnable fortress.

Another trading post frequented by the Nez Perce was Spokane House, located about a five-day horseback ride to the northwest from Stites and situated on the Spokane River. The post had been built in 1810 by Finan McDonald and Jaco

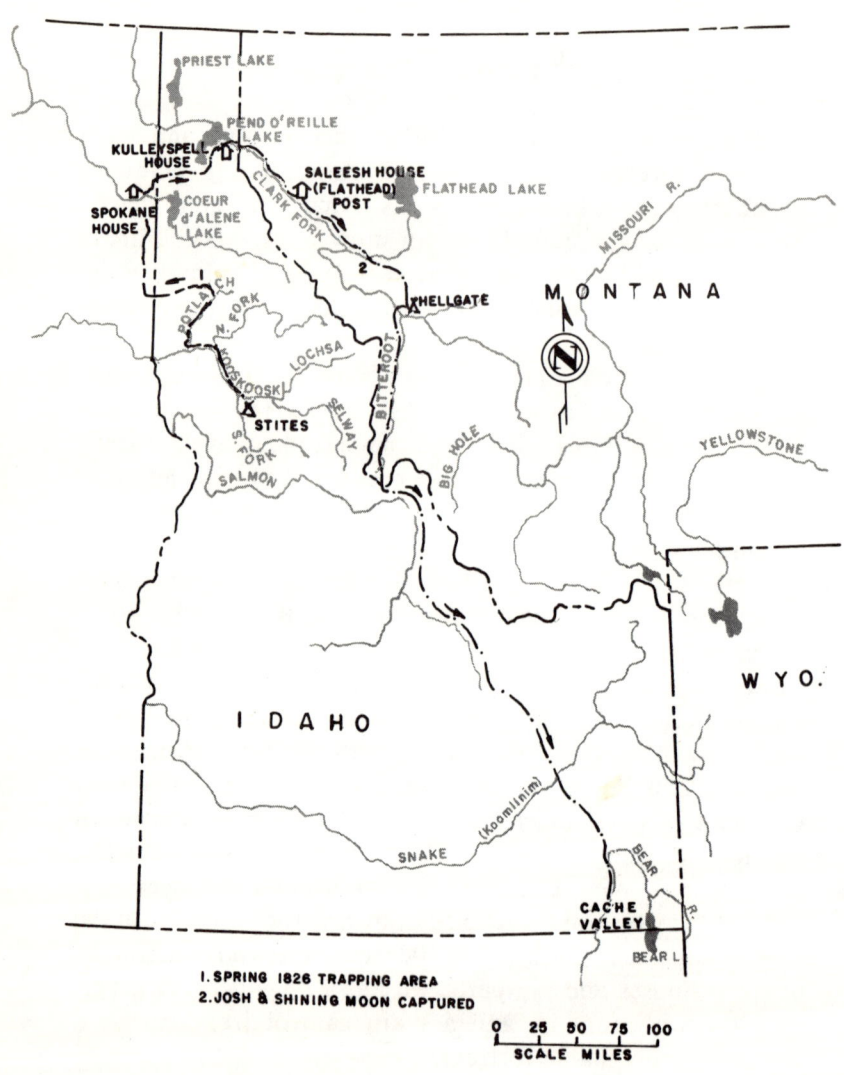

Spring, 1826, Adventures

Finlay of the North West Company. It, too, was accessible from Stites in the early spring months of March and April as there was little high country of consequence in between the two places where snow accumulated. The Nez Perce traded slaves, dried meat, furs, animal hides, elk teeth, camas roots, bear claws, baskets and corn grass with Wishram, Chinookian, Wasco, and Wanapum peoples at The Dalles and dried clams, fish oil, baskets, carved wooden implements, wappato roots, and dentalium shells from Vancouver Island. When the Nez Perce traveled east across the Bitterroot Mountains, they carried as trade goods dried berries, cakes of camas and kouse, horns of the bighorn mountain sheep, including bows, ladles, and spoons made from them, and also baskets made of cedar roots, arrows made from serviceberry, flat wallets of hemp and bear grass, horses, eagle feathers, salmon oil, dried salmon packed in salmon skin, dentalia and other sea shells they had acquired in trade with the coast Indians at The Dalles. They would trade for bone beads, horn spoons, pemmican, trunks and wallets of parfleche, buffalo robes — plain and ornamented with porcupine quills by Crow women — war bonnets made by Sioux Indians which had long double tails of eagle feathers.

* * *

With rendezvous time set for the last week of May in Cache Valley (was actually held in July) in northern Utah, Josh began making his preparations for travel. He made a trip up the South Fork of the Kooskooski River to recover his cached packs of beaver pelts. They were found to be in good condition, no worse for the winter's cache. Upon his return to Stites, he opened the packs and spread the furs out in the warm spring sun to dry and further cure.

While Josh was preparing for his departure, the Nez Perce were also preparing for travel. Some would go down the Columbia to trade at Fort Nez Perces. Others would visit neighboring tribes in their area of influence and still others would remain in Stites. In late May, most of the tribe which remained at Stites would move south up Cottonwood Creek and into the traditional camas meadows for a yearly supply of camas root which was an all-important staple in the diet of the

Nez Perce Indian and had been for many years. As the time of the camas digging came early in the summer and before forays by the war parties, many of the Nez Perce tribes got together at the camas meadows and while the women dug and prepared the camas cakes, the men would plot strategy for the summer.

The camas is a hyacinth-like wild lily with a tuberous plant which grows prolifically in the damp mountain meadows. The root looks somewhat like an onion, has a high starch content, and is prepared for eating by steaming. The women dig a pit in which they dump 20 to 25 bushels of camas roots on a bed of grass. Hot stones are placed over the roots and water poured over the rocks and then covered with dirt. The roots are allowed to slowly steam and cook for a day and a night after which they are taken from the hole and dried in the sun or made into small cakes and steamed again. The long cooking period breaks down the starch into sugar and the cooked camas has a taste somewhat like sweet potatoes.

Josh and Shining Moon departed the village at Stites on a warm spring day in early March, he riding his Appaloosa stallion, "Smoke" and she riding a pinto mare, trailed by the pack mule Midnight. They swam the river just above the confluence of the south fork with the middle fork of the Kooskooski. The water at this time of year was still low, as the snow in the high country had not yet started to melt. It would be June before the spring runoff would raise the river to its highest level from the melting of the deep snowpack.

They traveled down the north side of the river for one full day and until they came to the vicinity of Orofino Creek where they spent the night with a small group of Indians who were fishing for sturgeon in a deep eddy in the river located about a half mile above the mouth of the creek. The next morning, they departed the camp at daylight, again traveling down the north side of the river and within less than an hour came to the north fork, another large tributary of the Kooskooski, across which they swam their horses. Toward the end of the day, they came to the vicinity of the Nez Perce village of Cut Nose which was located just upriver at the mouth of the Potlatch River. Here they left the Kooskooski and traveled up the Potlatch, stopping at the small village of twenty lodges for a short time to speak to Chief Cut Nose and ask his permission to travel through his country and trap beaver. Josh had been told by Shining Moon that Red Eagle, younger son of Cut Nose, had made overtures toward marriage during the past winter, and that her father had refused the offer at her insistence, so it was prudent for Josh to be wary of this young Nez Perce warrior for he might decide to blame his failure in love on the mountain man and try to force a fight.

But the stories of the physical prowess of this huge mountain man and how he had single-handed rescued Shining Moon from the Pahkees had preceded him and had during the winter been the subject of discussion over many council fires. So young Red Eagle, while not afraid of this Long Knife, was smart enough to know his chances of survival in hand to hand combat were not to his advantage and for the moment restrained himself.

After smoking with Cut Nose the pipe filled with kinnikinnick, the inner bark of the red willow, and after much sign language and a few words in Nez Perce, the chief gave Josh permission to travel through and to trap in his country. The meeting was not without incident, as Red Eagle who was gaily attired in his war regalia and riding a beautiful white stallion painted with orange and red stripes, rode back and forth through the village displaying his displeasure at this mountain man taking the beaver from his country. Red Eagle felt as did most Nez Perce that the mountain man who trapped for the beaver was doing a squaw's work and he harangued and ridiculed the Long Knife.

Josh paid no attention to this young warrior, as he did not wish to incur the enmity of these people and so related his feelings to Chief Cut Nose. Josh told the chief that he knew what was motivating his son and admonished him for treating a proven friend of the Nez Perce in the manner he was displaying.

In exchange for the reasonable treatment and the permission to hunt in the Potlatch River country, Josh gave Chief Cut Nose a Hudson's Bay three-point blanket, one which he had long carried with him for just such an occasion.

Departing the Nez Perce village without having had a confrontation with Red Eagle, Josh and Shining Moon rode rapidly up the narrow valley of the Potlatch River. As evening

approached, they came to a sizeable side stream entering from the north known as Big Bear Creek. The Nez Perce traveled up Bear Creek to its headwaters to dig the white clay which they used to tan hides and make them white. They had told Josh of the many beaver in the country. Here they camped for the night in a brushy draw along the river just above the mouth of the stream. The steep hills that formed the Potlatch River Canyon were generally treeless at the lower elevations but covered with evergreen trees on the north-facing slopes and at the higher elevations. The grass on the south-facing slopes was beginning to turn green and the bushes in the wet draws were bursting with buds. The Potlatch River across which you could very easily throw a stone now carried the spring runoff of melting snow from its lowland headwaters. The water was now higher than at any other season of the year. The yellow orange-limbed but yet leafless willow, the budding aspen, and the cottonwood trees lined the stream.

Though they were camped supposedly in the country of the friendlies, Josh still took precaution to locate his camp where it could be defended if necessary. He was aware that Red Eagle just could yet make an attempt to gain redress for his supposed grievances, for he was hot tempered and could be expected to do the unexpected. He would, Josh knew, someday, somewhere, try to avenge the aggravated affront to his pride. He needed to prove himself, to exhibit his prowess. Where better to do it than against almost impossible odds.

Josh had observed beaver activity along Big Bear Creek and as evening approached set his six traps in likely locations along the stream. With the coming of morning, Josh's fear of attack during the night had not materialized but he had slept very lightly and was awake early to see the fading of the starlight and the graying of the sky in the east behind the high canyon walls across the river. Josh listened to the sounds of the wilderness and heard only the rippling of the stream, the movement of his riding animals, and the drumming of a ruffed grouse on a log in a neck of timber just above camp. He kissed the forehead of his wife of such a few short months and arose from his buffalo hide bed. His first chore was to look to his traps and he found, much to his satisfaction, two beaver and one otter in his sets. Josh hastily skinned out his catch and returned to camp to find Shining Moon saddled up and prepared to travel.

By evening, they had ridden about fifteen miles generally northward up Big Bear Canyon. Here the land leveled out into broad grassy meadows to either side of the stream. The terrain was gently rolling with only a few higher evergreen-covered mountains to the east and north. Here Josh found considerable beaver activity and chose to spend some time trapping.

Josh and Shining Moon spent the last week of March and the first two weeks of April trapping the headwaters of both Big Bear Creek and the Potlatch River, each of which headed in this relatively low-lying meadow country, trapping in meadows that in later years would be named Wet, Vassar, Smith, Hog, Moose, and Cougar Meadows. Life was comfortable and easy in spite of the cold wet spring and the snow that still lay in the shade under the trees and along the high ridges. This was virgin country and the trapping was good, for in three weeks Josh had caught fifty beaver and five otter. The worth of each otter was equal to two "made" beaver. At five or six dollars a beaver plew, Josh now had pelts enough to trade for all the powder, ball, and supplies he needed to sustain him until the rendezvous as well as buy Shining Moon foofaraw the likes of which she had never dreamed.

With enough pelts to trade for the supplies he needed, Josh chose to head his entourage west, skirting the mountains to the north. He traveled this route for a day and camped for the night on Paradise Creek where it came down from the mountain to the north. The contour of the mountain resembled a full-breasted sleeping Indian maiden and he laughingly compared it to Shining Moon. The stream circled the high ground in the valley between the hills and flowed toward the setting sun. Lush grass covered the hills which resembled sand dunes in shape. This was a beautiful valley in which many antelope roamed and when one inquisitive young buck came too close, Josh dropped him in his tracks and they had "goat" that night for dinner.

The expanse of open meadow in the valley was known by the Indians as Tat-kin-mah, meaning the home of the young and spotted deer. In the early summer months of May and June, the new green grass was a welcome food for the young fawns. The lower wet meadows, Josh noted, were covered with extensive growths of camas. The country would be in later years called "The Palouse," a land of lush grass and clear water.

The trail to the north and west was no longer blocked by high mountains and Josh and Shining Moon now followed the trail over rolling terrain toward the Hudson's Bay trading post at Spokane House located along the Spokane River near the mouth of the Little Spokane River. The trip of ninety miles took them three days after leaving the camp on Paradise Creek. They followed the prominent landmarks about which they had been told, including a high pointed conical butte rising well above the surrounding terrain which in later years would be named Steptoe Butte. The Indians used the butte as a lookout, for from the top one could see many miles in all directions.

Upon arriving in the vicinity of Spokane House, a trading post which had been built by the "Northwesters," Finan McDonald and Jaco Finlay in the spring of 1810, they found it to have been abandoned only recently. In fact, in talking with the friendly Spokane Indians in the area, Josh learned that only a day before he had arrived, on April 18, John Work, Francis Ermatinger, and Finan McDonald had started down the Spokane River with a boat load of furs and sundries bound for the new post in the Okanogan area at Colville.

Josh was chagrined that he had missed a chance to trade for supplies. However, from further questioning of the local Indians, he learned of another trading post located on the Clark Fork River known as Saleesh House (Flathead Post), one of several which had been originally constructed by the Northwesters and later run by the Hudson's Bay Company. David Thompson of the North West Company of Montreal had built the post in November of 1809 near Thompson Falls for trading with the Flathead Indians who lived in the area. Since the post lay astride the relatively snow-free water level trail into the buffalo country, the Nez Perce, Spokane, and Coeur d'Alene Indians frequently visited the fort.

The Blackfoot Indians soon got wind of the trading being carried on with other Indians and blocked the trail into the buffalo country from the Columbia Basin and for a period of time prevented further trade. The fort was abandoned for a time but was later reopened for trading.

The Spokane Indians also told Josh about another trading post, Kullyspell House on the east shore of Lake Pend Oreille, a large lake three days ride to the northeast. The fort was located where the Clark Fork River empties into the lake. The fort, however, had been abandoned soon after it had been built because of its proximity to Spokane House and of pressure from the Blackfoot. David Thompson had established both Saleesh House and Kullyspell House in 1809, and had operated them for trading with the Flathead, Nez Perce, and other Columbia Basin Indians. While Kullyspell was abandoned soon after it was established, Saleesh House was operated until 1821 by the North West Company, when the Hudson's Bay Company and the North West Company combined. It was then taken over by the Hudson's Bay people. It served as the post nearest the territory which had been purchased in 1803 from France by the United States as part of the Louisiana Purchase. The Hudson's Bay Company intended to use the post as the pivotal point from which they outfitted brigades to trap beaver.

Josh and Shining Moon arrived at Saleesh House on the evening of the 23rd of April, 1826. Although the British were hospitable, they were concerned by the appearance of an American in the country. They were usually hospitable, as it was not their way to appear other than friendly. However, the current policy of the HBC was to create a beaver desert, a scorched earth along the continental divide and thus eliminate the American threat of competition west of the divide and on into the Oregon country. They reasoned that if they could create an economic desert in the headwaters of the Kootenai, the Clark Fork, the Snake, the Salmon, the Blackfoot, the Bitterroot, and the Green Rivers, they could make it economically unfeasible for the Americans to move westward into the Oregon country and thus they would protect their interests there. All of the land south of the 49th parallel and west of the Rocky Mountains was disputed territory and included all of the modern states of Oregon, Washington, and Idaho. The country was by agreement occupied jointly by the United States and Britain. The people of the Hudson's Bay

Company had come to the realization that much of the country would probably be ceded to the United States in time, so they had developed a scorched earth plan. But from the beginning, the plan went awry. Jed Smith and six companions of the Ashley Fur Company had in the fall of 1824 encountered in the field Alexander Ross, a brigade leader of the Hudson's Bay Company and had followed him north to this same Saleesh House on the Clark Fork River. There they spent a part of the winter gaining considerable knowledge of the trading methods utilized by the Hudson's Bay people. They departed in December of 1824 with Peter Skene Ogden, another Hudson's Bay brigade leader and traveled back south toward the Green River and Bear Lake.

Peter Skene Ogden left Saleesh House (Flathead Post) on December 20, 1824 with a party of about 75 men, most of whom were Iroquois-French half-breeds. They carried 25 tipis, 80 rifles, 364 beaver traps, and 372 horses. From Flathead Post, they traveled eastward up the Clark Fork River to the vicinity of present-day Missoula, Montana, "Hellgate," and southward up the Bitterroot River, over Lost Trail Pass, and south into Idaho to the Salmon River and from there into the headwaters of the Snake and on deeper into jointly held territory. Ogden had crossed the continental divide when he crossed into the headwaters of the Snake and into what was American territory. Jed Smith followed Ogden south on his way to the Bear Lake area, the vicinity in which the 1825 rendezvous would be held and where other future rendezvous would occur.

Josh and Shining Moon spent only as much time at Saleesh House as was necessary to obtain information concerning the trail to the south and to exchange the beaver pelts for the necessities of the trail and some foofaraw for Shining Moon. This was the first chance that Josh had had to buy his wife the things that he knew would make her eyes light up like a firefly on a hot night in July. There was vermilion for her cheeks, red ribbon for her hair, a red Hudson's Bay three-point blanket for a wrap, and calico for a dress with hawk bells for decoration.

Josh traded only as many of his newly-caught plews as was necessary to satisfy his immediate needs, for he was a patriotic frontier American and remembered very well his parents talking about the Revolutionary War and he wanted as little as possible to do with the British who were trespassing on American territory. Besides, the British did not pay as well for pelts as did the Americans.

Josh and Shining Moon rode away from Saleesh House with Josh mulling over in his mind his reaction to the British, while Shining Moon was thinking of the many new baubles they had traded for.

The trip on the well-traveled trail up the Clark Fork River from Lake Pend Oreille to Saleesh House had been without incident as the Flathead Indians living in the area were friendly to the white man. Up to now they had ridden without much danger, but now that they were beyond the area of influence of the British and were riding deeper into the Bitterroot Range, they were in the home land of the Blackfoot Indians. With Shining Moon to look after, Josh became very apprehensive about following the well-worn and easy trail up the river. They were, however, forced to follow the river because of the deep snow in the mountains which rose to snowy heights immediately on either side of the river. This trail, Josh knew, could serve as a well-baited trap and two people would have little chance against a well-planned ambush. Travel could continue only after he had scouted the trail ahead. It was the only logical way, so Josh rode ahead and if after a period of time he did not give an alarm, Shining Moon would follow with the animals. Using this procedure in the obvious places of ambush and by riding at night, they arrived at the confluence of the Flathead River without incident. They chose to travel up the Flathead to bypass the big "S" in the Clark Fork River as it breached the Bitterroot Mountains. About fifteen miles up the Flathead, the valley widens out and the range of treeless hills falls away from the river to the north. To the south, however, the ponderosa pine-covered mountains rise to an elevation of nearly eight thousand feet.

Josh surveyed the trail to the southeast and up the Flathead River and could find no recent sign of Indians moving through the country. They continued their travel up the trail until it entered open country where he could see clearly for about three miles up the river. It was nearing evening and they chose to camp up a small creek, Seeray Creek, running into the river from the south and rising on Burnt Fork Pinnacle in the range of mountains to the south, the range that separated the Clark Fork River from the Flathead River. To avoid leaving readable sign, they rode above the mouth of the stream for a quarter of a mile and then swam down the river and waded ashore and up the stream bed of Seeray Creek. They rode up the stream until they came to a meadow in which grew a heavy growth of willow along the stream. It was in these willows they set up camp.

Shining Moon made camp and set about getting something to eat while Josh went upstream from camp to set the tethers and hobbles on the horses. Josh felt a cool breeze on his face and looked skyward to see low clouds scudding by the tops of the high peaks. It would rain tonight, he mused to himself. He would keep the stock close to camp in case of a severe spring storm. They had a long trip ahead of them and he did not wish to chance the loss of their animals. Even though the stock needed to graze after a long day on the trail, it was better to have a hungry horse than no horse at all.

Josh was about to finish tying the rawhide hobbles on old Midnight, the pack mule, when he felt her stiffen, snort, and swing her gaze toward camp. He was instantly alert to the presence of hostiles, even though he had seen no recent sign of travelers along the trail. He knew this lack of sign did not always tell of the presence of those wily wilderness inhabitants, for they, too, survived by their wits in this most fearsome land.

Josh finished tying the hobbles on Midnight's front feet and picked up his Hawken and walked rapidly but stealthily back toward the camp in the willows. He sniffed the air, but in the evening the direction of the air currents was downstream toward the camp and he could detect only the smell of his horses and no other unusual odors. He thought it possible that he was begging trouble. Had he been alone, he would have made himself scarce until he could determine what frightened the mule. However, he continued approaching the camp.

When he walked into the camp perimeter, he looked around for Shining Moon and did not find her beside the small aspen wood fire. She must have gone to the nearby stream for water, he thought. He listened for her footsteps but did not hear her moccasined feet, so he softly called her name and got no answer.

Josh surveyed the ground for sign of her departure from the camp and read sign that told him that she had been forcibly taken from the camp by several moccasin-footed Indians. It was then that he detected movement in the willows and before he could defend himself, he was surrounded by several painted Blackfoot warriors, each carrying a North West trade fusee, some of which were pointed at Josh's chest. At the moment, the thought ran through his mind how was it that he had not detected them and how was it that he had been caught so unaware of their presence? The leader of the group was a relatively young, short, muscular Indian who had black piercing eyes and a hard-set jaw. He walked toward Josh and made sign for him to drop his rifle, his knife, and his fire bag. They then tied Josh's hands behind his back and motioned for him and Shining Moon to lie face down on the ground.

For a time, the Blackfeet sorted through the furs and other paraphenalia, all the while chattering about their fortunate capture. The chief whom they later learned was named Winter Bull took charge of the booty, rounded up their horses, and tried to load the spoils of capture on old Midnight who immediately bucked them off. Josh had to smile to himself at her actions. Even in this predicament, he could hardly constrain himself to keep from laughing.

After loading their ill-gotten gains on one of their own horses, the party moved down the creek to the Flathead River, traveling along the river through the night until they came to the confluence of the Jocko River which enters the Flathead where it turns sharply north toward Flathead Lake. Here they stopped for a time for rest and something to eat.

After a stop of two hours, the troop continued up the Jocko River until they came to a low pass through the mountains to the south. They swung into the pass and traveled for about ten miles until they came into a wide valley surrounded by high mountains through which a large river flowed which Josh presumed was again the Clark Fork River.

In the valley near the junction of another large stream, Josh saw the encampment of about forty tipis. These proved to be the camp of Winter Bull. Their entry into the camp was one of excitement for not only did they have two prisoners, the party was returning from trading at Flathead Post. There they had traded their fall and winters' catch of furs and hides for much-needed supplies. It had been while they were in the vicinity of the post that they had seen Josh and Shining Moon and had trailed them up the Clark Fork and to their camp on Seeray Creek, waiting for the opportunity to present itself to capture the pair without injury to themselves. As long as Josh and Shining Moon had traveled east toward their camp, Winter Bull had felt no urgency to move in for the capture.

Josh and Shining Moon were paraded through the camp and exhibited before the tribal members who jeered, poked, and jabbed at the prisoners. Josh had been stripped of all of his equipment and all of his clothes and Shining Moon had been relieved of all of the foofaraw which she had so recently acquired.

Chief Winter Bull watched the two prisoners and meditated on what they would do with them. He had been very much taken by the beauty of this Nez Perce woman and entertained thoughts of taking her for his own. She was, by right of capture, his slave and he could do with her as he so desired.

As for the huge Long Knife, the chief was undecided as to whether he should submit him to as many indignities as he could think of before turning him over to the squaws to mutilate, torture, and slowly kill, or, should he run the Long Knife through the gauntlet and weaken him slowly with massive physical torture and when he was sufficiently weak, Winter Bull would engage him in personal combat with weapons of his own choosing, possibly a knife or a club or an axe and do the killing himself? The chief decided on the latter course of action.

Sixth Interlude
Beliefs

While the Indian held contempt for anyone who showed fear or pain, he held great admiration for those who exhibited courage. He often permitted his prisoners the chance to escape, if by so doing, he showed outstanding courage. Involved also was the contest of pitting the physical prowess of the captive against that of the Indian. It gave the latter the chance to exhibit his courage and skill, albeit from a position of strength.

Such was the reason for what to the white man was the seemingly strange exhibition of courage by the Indian. One of these exhibitions was that of permitting a captive to run the gauntlet. The members of the tribe would align themselves in two parallel lines, each person armed with a weapon capable of inflicting an incapacitating wound on the unfortunate captive. If the captive survived the run between the lines of savages, each member of which was intent on dealing a fatal blow, and then could outrun his captors and not be wounded beyond recovery out in the wilderness, he might live to tell the tale.

The Indian also believed that in a duel the victor inherited the honors that had been held by his adversary. The things that were important to an Indian were the Medicine, his honor, his status and acceptance among his fellow warriors, and to count coup, to show physical prowess in battle, to ignore pain, and to scalp an enemy.

There were two ways that an Indian believed he could prevent an enemy from reaching the happy hunting grounds and thus never encounter him in the hereafter. One was by scalping his enemy, for the spirit of the vanquished at that time ceased to exist, and could never pass on to that sought-for paradise. A second way was for the Indian to die by strangulation. His spirit could not then escape from his body as he believed that it passed through the mouth. Thus the Indian feared death by hanging.

Visualizing why the Indian society believed in such extreme

life or death measures is not difficult. Life itself in the wilderness was tenuous and filled with many dangers, and in accepting these dangers, the Indian resolved to face all adversity with courage and without fear. As a direct result of this extreme existence, the Indian developed an appropriate set of values. He held and exhibited no compassion and would inflict on an enemy any indignity he could in an attempt to make him show fear or to cry out for mercy. He prided himself on his contempt for pain and believed that by dying in battle he enhanced his chance for a life hereafter. Self torture was not unusual in the Indian society. Part of the ritual of the Sun Dance performed by some tribes included self torture. When a young man was promoted to the rank of warrior, he participated in a bloody ordeal. In this rite, a knife was passed behind the muscles of the chest and the flesh lifted from the bone. Horsehair ropes were tied through and behind the muscles and the other ends tied high on a lodge pole. The candidate warrior must free himself from this tether by tearing the flesh. He was allowed no food or water and if during the ordeal he showed any sign of pain he would be released and thereafter be a disgraced man. He could neither marry nor hold property and was required thereafter to do a squaw's work. The Indian was so thoroughly imbued with this cult of peer esteem that his whole existence was pervaded by complete dedication to its principles.

While he generally held no reverence for a superior creator, the Indian was much concerned with his existence relative to the elements of nature, to his fellow warriors, and to the unexplained occurrences in his daily life. These unaccountable mysterious happenings were resolved through complete dedication to making Medicine. The warrior carried with him at all times a Medicine bag in which were items which when mixed together and possibly tossed to the four winds or tied in a small bundle and attached to the tail of his war horse could bolster the personality of the warrior and quell his superstitions. Other items which could be found in the bag were bones or portions of birds, animals, or reptiles. There could be colored sand or dirt and when mixed together in a container would constitute good Medicine. In fact, the Indian did not make a move without first making Medicine, or of consulting his own personal Wyakin, or if his personal Medicine failed, he might consult a medicine man, or shaman, for advice.

Pipe smoking occupied a very important place in the ritualistic existence of the Indian. He always smoked the pipe in public and never while he was alone. It was a breach of decorum for a person in an assemblage to refuse to smoke the pipe. There were pipes for all occasions and special events. There were peace pipes, medicine pipes, council pipes, and pipes for everyday uses. The special pipes were used only on the occasion for which the pipe was reserved.

To the white man, probably one of the most unbelievable of the beliefs of the Indian was that of "counting coup." It consisted of the act of either riding or running up to an enemy during a battle and touching him with a coup stick and then trying to escape alive.

Such an act was one which deserved the highest honors. A victim killed in battle was claimed by the first warrior to touch him with his coup stick and he alone then had the right to scalp the body and strip it of its weapons and belongings.

Chapter 7
Pahkees

The racing feet of the mountain man were pin-cushioned by the needle-sharp spines of the prickly pear cactus, a pain-dealing obstacle that he had no time to avoid in his headlong flight to escape the now trailing but tenacious Blackfoot. Only the mental discipline developed from years of living in the wilderness and from the numbness brought on by desperation enabled Josh to endure the consuming pain which wracked his body. The hot, late afternoon April sun shone into his eyes and sweat ran from his still intact scalp down his face and body in enervating rivulets. The gnarled and shagbark limbs of the stunted dry-land brush clutched at his bare legs, tearing his flesh, and adding to the numerous abrasions and bruises he had absorbed in his dash for freedom through the gauntlet. His mouth, throat, and lungs, dehydrated by the searing, gasping breaths to sustain his knotting and cramping muscles cried out for moisture.

He wanted to stop, to lie down and rest, to succumb to the desire of his mind to lapse into unconsciousness and erase this immense pain which coursed in waves through his body, but he knew he must fight off this desire of his mind to escape from reality for he must prevent his being recaptured by the bloodthirsty savages, a capture from which he knew he would not survive. The enraged Blackfeet would subject him to such heinous torture that he would be unable to endure the pain and suffering without emotion. His death would also mean a life of slavery for Shining Moon. It was the Indian women who were the most vicious. The stories told around the campfires of the mountain men often dealt with the extreme limits to which the squaws would go in dealing out torture, for they were as cruel and obdurate as the men. They would thrust sharpened sticks into the prisoner's body just far enough so that the wounds were not fatal. They would heap red-hot coals on the spread-eagled and outstretched body, they would slash the body with knives, cut off the eyelids and pinion the body in the sun, cut off one's fingers and toes one at a time, break the large bones in the body by dropping huge rocks on the arms and legs, and when it seemed that the unfortunate prisoner was about to succumb from the torture, to commit one of the greatest indignities of all, to cut off the prisoner's testicles and stuff them into his mouth.

As Josh neared the Clark Fork River, he was aware that he could not run much farther and he looked around for a place to hide from his pursuers who now trailed him by about a quarter of a mile. He had been running for almost thirty minutes and must have covered four or five miles. He was completely exhausted and had fallen several times during the past ten minutes. However, his pursuers led by Chief Winter Bull were in no better condition for Josh had seen him stumble and fall on several occasions.

As Josh, naked and exhausted, ran parallel to the river, he saw ahead an extra large beaver lodge in a pond formed by a dam in a side stream. The agonizing pain in his body forced through his mind the thought of immediate escape and the beaver lodge provided a possible solution to his problem. Josh decided to dive into the pond and try to come up inside the lodge through the narrow underwater entrance. Such a move might just fool the Blackfeet if he could get inside the lodge without disturbing the muddy bottom of the pond or even if he did muddy the water, the Indians just might think that the muddy water had been made by a beaver.

Josh ran across the face of the dam to leave a trail for his pursuers to follow and when he reached the outcropping of rock on the far bank he dove into the pond and swam strongly underwater the fifty feet to the refuge of sticks and mud. His lungs were bursting for need of air and with the lodge between him and his pursuers, he pushed his head above the surface of the pond. He breathed deeply before he again dove to search for one of the two entrances to the lodge. Then with only moments to spare before the Indians would come into sight of the pond, Josh swam along the edge of the lodge searching for the opening. When he thought he could not stay under any longer, he discovered an opening and found it large enough into which he could squeeze his large body. He forced himself up through the passage, scraping the sides of the narrow opening, until his head broke through the surface of the water inside the lodge.

He pulled himself up on the mud shelf built up just above water level and lay there exhausted, breathing deeply of the musty stale air and listening for sounds of his pursuers. There was enough light transmitted through the two greenish-colored openings to permit limited vision and Josh looked about and found the living space uninhabited, for which he was thankful, for at this point he did not care to fight an old tom beaver for his home.

If the Indians would just believe that he had continued his overland flight or possibly that he had tried to swim the river, there just might be a chance that he would survive.

The living space in the lodge was large enough to permit him to lift most of his body out of the water, for the spring runoff was icy cold and he was soon wracked with spells of shivering and shaking. Although physically inured to the cold temperatures by long hours of setting and lifting traps in cold icy water, he was now exhausted from the ordeal he had just experienced and the shock of the icy cold water on his hot sweating body punished Josh severely. One thing the water had done, however, was quench the great thirst that Josh had developed from the long run, and the cold water did sooth the painful wounds he had received running the gauntlet and the exhausting run for his life.

It was not long before Josh could hear the muffled sounds of yelling Blackfeet as they searched the vicinity of the beaver dam. He could hear them crossing the dam and was aware that they had not picked up his trail beyond the far side of the dam. He knew that they would search up and down the river bank for miles. As the daylight waned and the sounds of pursuit diminished, Josh began to feel reassured and wanted to leave this welcome but icy cold refuge and seek a warmer abode. He knew he had no way to start a fire, neither did he have a gun or a knife with which to obtain food. Thoughts of how he might warm himself by burying himself in the sand or by covering up with leaves coursed through his mind. He was also aware of a consuming hunger as he had not eaten since early in the morning.

As darkness spread its friendly soft velvet cloak over the wilderness, Josh listened intently to detect any sounds of his pursuers, but the noises of the night told him that he was alone. He slid his tortured body into the water and through the passage and swam quietly to the shore. After listening again and smelling the air, he climbed from the pond and walked the short distance down the streambed to the Clark Fork. He waded into the river and swam downstream, staying under the surface as much as possible. When he felt he must come up for air, he turned on his back and floated to the surface and as quietly as possible pushed his head above water. After swimming for what he thought was about a mile or thereabouts, he turned toward the south bank of the river and when he was close enough to shore so that he could stand on the bottom, he looked around and listened and could detect no presence of the Blackfeet. It was during the dark of the moon which made it difficult to see beyond the edge of the stream, but the darkness was also his ally. He could dimly see the outline of the trees along the banks and the surrounding mountains were softly outlined against the bright stars in the southern sky.

Josh climbed out of the river onto the gravelly bank where the cottonwood trees formed a thicket near the water. He was in unfamiliar country and he knew he must reconnoiter his position and determine the lay of the land before moving from the river, for he did not wish to make a trail which could be followed without his knowing something about the territory. He crawled into the thicket, making as sure as he could that he did not leave a readable track. He dug a hole beside a large cottonwood log with a stick and his bare hands and lined it with grass and leaves. Covering himself with sand, leaves, and grass, he almost immediately sank into deep sleep in the newly found warmth.

The temperature at dawn was nearly freezing and the cold of the high mountain morning awakened Josh from his tormented sleep. He lay there quietly listening to the sounds of the grayish dawn, searching for those noises that would tell him that he was alone in the wilderness. He heard the howls of the coyote pups as they yipped their early morning cry for their mother to bring them some food and heard the faint cluck-cluck of the ruffed grouse as it began its early morning search for a breakfast of tender clover. All seemed serene, at least for the moment. Josh pushed the grass away from his face and looked up at an almost gray sky fading in the east to a lighter bluish gray. The stars were slowly being extinguished by a sun rising from behind the high mountains beyond the Hellgate to the east.

   Josh knew that when the sun cast its light on the high peaks of the Bitterroot Mountains to the west that the Blackfeet would again swarm over the wilderness searching for his trail. He also knew that when he did leave his hiding place, he would need to call on all of his wilderness skill to keep from being once again made their captive.

   It was then that he heard the rumble of many hundreds of trampling feet running toward his hiding place and finally decided it was a small herd of buffalo heading for the river, that had probably been disturbed by the Blackfeet. The thicket in which he was hidden was directly in the path of the stampeding buffalo and he would have probably been trampled had he not prepared his bed up against the large log. Their headlong flight was detoured around the log and he was not injured. After they had plunged into and swum the river, Josh was more at ease about his hiding place in the thicket. Any trail that he had made up from the river would have been obliterated by the buffalo and he could spend the day in relative safety from the searching Indians. He resolved to stay right where he was and try during the coming night to escape from his pursuers. Morning passed into afternoon and his place of refuge was not approached. The searching savages were apparently concentrating their efforts in the vicinity of the beaver dam. There had been a few mounted warriors riding by, but no one had approached his hiding place. The searchers always rode along the river bank and, thanks to the buffalo, had not picked up his trail. There were thousands of places where the Long Knife could have hidden and their best chance was to some way pick up his trail to follow. Before the day was over, the Blackfeet appeared to be giving up the search, for Josh had not seen or heard any Indians for some time. Even the riders who had searched farther down the river had long since ridden back toward the village to the east.

The heat of the afternoon sun that filtered down into his hiding place felt good to Josh and warmed his body, but the ants, buffalo flies, and mosquitoes were troublesome and he had difficulty keeping his movements at a minimum and only the fact that he was partially covered with sand was he able to generally ignore the pests.

As the day wore on and the evening approached, Josh had studied the terrain as best he could from his vantage point and had settled on a route of escape. He would not, as he strongly desired to do, return to the vicinity of the village and try to rescue Shining Moon and his equipment. He would instead head for the high country to the north and attempt to snare animals for food and clothing, bide his time, and try to catch a lone Indian rider out away from the village and regain a knife, a gun, and possibly a horse. However, it would be much easier to hide without a horse and he would concentrate on the utensils with which to fight and obtain food.

With the coming of darkness and with the stars to give him direction, Josh moved out of the thicket which had served to protect him for the day and waded into the river and swam to the north shore. He then traveled north for about three miles into the high mountains up Ninemile Creek toward Nine Mile Ridge. By midnight, he had climbed upward until he came to Six Mile Creek and then up it northwestward toward Squaw Peak.

Traveling at night was difficult at best and when Josh felt that he was far enough up Six Mile Creek, he climbed out of the stream bed onto a log that had fallen across the stream, walked through the underbrush on the log, and proceeded up the side hill on a matted bed of fallen ponderosa pine needles. He walked up a ridge until he came to a blown down tree into which he decided to crawl and spend the remainder of the night. He laid himself down on a bed of pine needles and listened to the noises of the night to determine who his neighbors might be. It was then that he noticed how hungry he was. He had drunk huge draughts of water as he had climbed up the canyon, but that had only partially satisfied his great hunger. He had not eaten for two days and he was aware that come morning he must devise some way to trap or snare some small animals for food and clothing.

After a cold and fretful night's sleep, Josh awoke with the dawn, listened to its sounds, and hearing none that he deemed dangerous to his person, he was about to get up from his leafy bed, when he could hardly believe his eyes for there not ten feet from his head stood a foolhen, a Franklin's grouse, eyeing him first with one red-circled eye and then, turning its head, with the other eye. Now a foolhen will do strange things. On some occasions, it will fly when approached and on others it will run along the ground. It is a clumsy bird and often can be easily dispatched with a rock or a stick. Josh moved his eyes around searching for a rock or a stick with which to obtain a much-needed meal. He finally decided on a broken limb lying just beside his hand. He then debated whether he should move rapidly or slowly. He chose to move slowly, to pick up the stick, and hope that he did not scare the bird into flight. Well, the final outcome was good for the man and poor for the bird, but it did provide Josh with his first meal in two days, albeit a raw one. It did not take him long to clean up all but the bones and the feathers.

During the following two days, Josh traveled eastward, staying in the high country, catching fish or a rabbit now and then, digging the roots of the ground nut, peeling and eating the cambrium of the deciduous bushes, and consuming blossoms and leaves of the clover. He found patches of wild onions, dug and ate the roots of the biscuitroot, the lomatiums, and dined on wild celery, cattails, mountain sorrel, lemon grass, and watercress. Most of the berries had not ripened and he subsisted on greens, roots, and the uncooked flesh of the fish, rabbits, and small game he could snare, snares that he constructed of spruce roots. He set them along well-traveled rabbit trails and at the entrances to small animal's burrows. The center of the loop was set at about the level of a small animal's head and when the animal was snared, its struggling tightened the loop. The end of the loop was often tied to a twitch-up made by bending a small tree or bush under a forked stick. The struggling of the animal released the tree and the animal was suspended in the air by its neck.

Josh caught fish by using thorns as hooks on which he threaded a worm or an insect for bait. His fishline he made by plaiting strands of hair pulled from his own head. It did not take him long to catch enough snowshoe hares and ground squirrels, the skins of which he made into a skin suit using spruce roots (watap) for thread. By punching holes in the skins and threading the stringy spruce roots through the holes, it wasn't long before he tailored for himself a suit and some moccasins made from rabbit and ground squirrel hides. Although the suit was hot during the day, Josh was glad to have some protection from the sun and from the chill of the night. The skins were also welcome during the evening and the nights, for he needed protection from insects, particularly the "no-see-ums" which were the worst during the evening.

Almost ten days had now elapsed since he had escaped from the Blackfeet and while he had survived by his hard-earned knowledge of the outdoors, he was desirous of a cooked meal and for some clothing more suitable to his needs. He also wanted to return to the vicinity of the Blackfoot village and try to rescue his wife and possibly retrieve some of his lost possessions. To satisfy either of these desires would be risky and would take considerable planning and lots of luck.

Josh was aware of the fact that his wife would be watched very closely if she were still alive, and to be successful, he would probably need to spend a large part of the summer or even the winter awaiting the chance to make a rescue attempt. But first things first, he would need weapons of some nature with which to hunt for food and clothing. And so he bent his efforts in that direction. He mulled over the alternatives which he had to obtain weapons and garments. One option was to travel back down the Clark Fork to Flathead Post and ask for the stake of an outfit from the British which he could repay with beaver pelts. While this plan would probably be the surest way of outfitting himself, Josh was reluctant to make himself subservient to the British and he had really not satisfied himself as to whether the Blackfeet had not been assisted in some way by the people at Flathead Post in his being captured in the first place. He had no pelts to trade and if he accepted the equipment he would then be beholden to them, a condition he did not relish. He was fiercely loyal to the United States and even though he had traded a few of his pelts to the Hudson's Bay traders, he had given only what was necessary to re-outfit himself for the trip to the Ashley fur company rendezvous.

Josh thought about the low pass through which they had traveled just north of the Blackfoot village that connected the valley of the Flathead with that of the Clark Fork. The Blackfeet apparently used the pass extensively on their travels to the north and west. The pass was a water course that was narrow and presented many places where an ambush could be set up. Josh decided to watch it for a time and observe the nature of the travel. The pass was located about ten miles north of where the Bitterroot River meets the Clark Fork. From his vantage position on the high ridge overlooking the Clark Fork valley, Josh could see a wide expanse of country to the south and east and did on occasion see riders approaching the pass who were traveling north into the country of the Flathead River and the Flathead Lake which lay about seventy miles to the north. It was here that Josh decided to set his trap and ambush some unfortunate savage and take from him his utensils of survival, his rifle, knife, flint, and steel.

For the next two days, Josh reconnoitered the pass from one end to the other. It was about seven miles long and he finally decided that the south entrance provided the best place to set his vigil. He would, he determined, wait for a lone rider traveling north and try to ambush him as he rode the trail into the steep-walled canyon. The rider would be particularly wary as he rode into the canyon from the valley and any ambush would need to be well planned and skillfully executed. For a time, Josh mulled over in his mind a suitable plan. He discarded several ideas that came to him, but finally decided that his best weapon was the element of surprise. He would attract attention of the rider away from his ambush position and while the Indian was absorbed in the distraction, he would unhorse him by attacking from a hidden position in the opposite direction and hope to subdue him before he could recover and retaliate. It was absolutely necessary that his plan be as foolproof as possible, for once he was recognized, he would once again be pursued relentlessly until he was again captured and he would not be given another chance to escape.

The reaction of an Indian who has been brought up in the wilderness is not always easy to predict and Josh could only speculate on what would happen in such an encounter.

However, he proceeded to set up his ambush with meticulous care. He knew from his experience when he had rescued Shining Moon from the Blackfeet previously that a surprised Indian is a howling, confused individual and he would have that period of time to press his advantage. He would try to make use of the fact that the Indian would be particularly attentive to his surroundings at the time he rode into the narrow canyon. The place Josh selected for the ambush was at a creek crossing along the trail where the Indian would be looking down into the ford, just before dropping into the stream. The trail turned sharply at this point, but there was a good line of sight almost fifty yards in either direction, giving Josh plenty of time to set up his ambush when that one Indian came through the canyon.

He would prepare a "twitch-up" with a trip vine trigger which could be quickly set up if and when he saw a lone rider coming along the trail. Josh spent several hours meticulously preparing his ambush. He located the hiding place from which he would mount his attack regardless of the direction from which the rider would come. He would prefer that the rider come from the south because he would have more time to prepare the ambush, since he could see farther in that direction. Waiting for the right situation might take days, but he was a patient man and would not be hasty in picking the right situation.

Josh decided that the hill located in the middle of the south entrance to the pass would provide an excellent place to view the trail in the canyon to the north as well as the open approach from the valley to the south.

Knowing that once he had prepared his ambush and he had spent hours erasing any sign that he had left, he would need to take with him up on the hill enough food to sustain himself for several days. To satisfy his thirst, he could climb down during the night to the stream in the canyon well away from the trail.

From his observation point, Josh saw several parties of Indians, sometimes in groups of three or four, and on occasions in larger groups, but for three days there had not been any lone riders on the trail. While time was an element in his life, and he fretted for his wife, Josh was aware of the need for patience and awaited another dawn in hopes of accomplishing his goal.

With the coming of the morning of the fourth day, only the voice of the wind disturbed a quiet as silent as the passing of the dawn, and as Josh looked at the sky, he saw the high cirrus clouds that resembled horse's tails which to anyone who was a student of the outdoors foretold of the storm to come. Josh was chewing some dried rabbit meat, as he moved silently from his bed in a serviceberry thicket to his vantage point to again set his vigil and watch the trail through the early morning mists that hung in the draws and valleys. As he watched almost absent mindedly a wren hopping about in the low branches of the serviceberry bushes searching for its breakfast, he looked up from the wren and through the mist to the south saw three animals, two horses with riders and the third a pack animal, approach the pass up from the open slopes in the valley. The leader of the two riders was mounted on a horse that for some reason or other looked strangely familiar to Josh. He watched the pair intently as they drew nearer to the pass and soon he was almost sure that the lead rider was Winter Bull, riding his gray Appaloosa stallion, Buffalo Horse, that Black Elk had given him, that Winter Bull had taken from him when he was captured. The second rider was following close behind the lead horse on an animal that appeared to be tied with a rawhide tether to the lead horse. Following the two horses was, and Josh could never mistake her, Midnight, the pack mule. The second Indian seemed to ride as though bound and tied to the saddle horn by a short rope. Then it came to Josh. The second rider was Shining Moon. Winter Bull was taking his pelts and his wife somewhere to trade them. Possibly to the Blackfoot villages to the north on Flathead Lake? To the British at Flathead Post? The pelts and Shining Moon would bring lots of whiskey at Flathead Post or many horses from some young Blackfoot warrior.

"Well, ticks on my pizzle!" said Josh under his breath.

To have his possessions all right there before him with only one adversary, Winter Bull, standing between him and all that meant anything to him in the world, was almost unbelievable. The circumstances were perfect and he cautiously proceeded toward his prepared ambush.

Seventh Interlude
Indian Foods

An adequate food supply and a protective shelter are necessary elements in the survival of man in any civilization. The pre-Columbian plateau Indians who chose the intermountain area of the northwestern United States as their home, settled along the Columbia River and its tributaries because the waters provided them with a continued replenished food supply — several separate runs of anadromous salmon and also the sea-run rainbow trout. These fish returned by the thousands to the same streams in which they were spawned, thereby a supply of food was assured and could be depended on year after year.

This replenished food supply permitted the plateau Indian to establish a relatively permanent residence, the pit house, in which they lived year after year. Each year the life-sustaining salmon first appeared in the streams early in the summer. The event was looked forward to with great anticipation. To the Nez Perce Indian it was the "hillal" — the coming of the first salmon. Lookouts were posted along the streams and it was an honor to be the first to see a fish "nosing" its way upstream or along the weirs placed in the riffles in the streams — weirs built to impede the progress of the fish long enough for the Indian to spear or trap them. With the fresh salmon there would be feasting in the village after a long winter of often short rations.

Those Indians living along the larger and deeper tributaries traveled long distances to the rapids and falls in the rivers where the salmon were forced to jump out of the water to climb the rapids. Such a place was the Dalles, a low falls in the lower Columbia River. Here the Indians built scaffolds out over the falls and with long handled nets caught the salmon as they attempted to jump the falls. Food gathering was a family affair even though several families would cooperate in building the weirs placed in the river behind which the salmon were speared or trapped. The men caught the salmon and the women would split and hang them on drying racks built over pits in which fires were kept burning to smoke the fish.

The salmon comprised over half of the food eaten by the northwest plateau Indian. The "runs" were almost continuous from late spring through early winter and smoked, the fish were stored in caches for several months. There were three distinct runs of Chinook salmon, first of which was a spring run arriving in the smaller tributaries in late May and early June. There was a mid-summer run arriving in the streams in July and August, and a third run composed of large fish which spawned for the most part in the larger rivers. The sea-run rainbow trout, the steelhead, began appearing in the streams in October and November and stayed in the rivers over the winter to spawn in April.

During most years, the larger streams did not freeze over and fishing could be carried on almost continuously. While the salmon would spawn and die soon after arriving in the streams, the steelhead lived all winter in the river, spawned in April and returned to the ocean or stayed in the stream to spawn another year. It was during the particularly cold winters when the streams were frozen and the Indian could not fish that famine haunted the the Indians. Without a supply of fresh fish, the supply of cached smoked fish was soon exhausted and Indians were forced to search for other sources of food. It was in the late winter before the root-bearing plants began to grow that the Indian faced famine.

While the Indian was a good shot with a bow and arrow, the animals, the deer, the elk, the bighorn mountain sheep, the mountain goats, the antelope, and the bear were difficult to hunt during the winter because of deep snow in the mountains. Animals living in the vicinity of the villages were hunted vigorously and soon eradicated.

It was with the coming of spring when the sun thawed the south and west facing slopes that the first plants began to appear. One of the early plants which the Indians looked for and dug was the kouse plant. The tuberous root of the kouse plant was edible and relished by the Indian. Kouse roots were collected and boiled into mush. The mush could be eaten immediately or baked into a form of bread or biscuit which could be stored for future use. The bread tasted like stale wheat flour biscuits. The early white explorers called the kouse plants "biscuit root."

During the months of May and June, the blue blossomed, hyacinth-like wild lily, the camas, appeared in the poorly-drained mountain meadows. The Indians traveled to these meadows yearly and dug the bulbous roots by the bushel. The roots were high in starch content and when steam-cooked the starch was transformed into sugar. The camas roots were cooked in a large pit, the bottom and sides of which were lined with grass. Hot rocks were dropped into the pit, and buckets of peeled camas roots dumped into the pit. Water was then poured into the pit. The grass and leaves covered the roots and dirt was thrown into the pit to contain the steam. A fire was then built on the dirt. In about 24 hours the cooked camas roots were uncovered and taken from the pit, some of which would be eaten initially, and some dried in the sun. Others were pounded into a meal and made into cakes. The cakes would be steamed a second time. The starch in the root was converted into sugar and they tasted somewhat like a sweet potato.

Later in the summer, wild berries were added to the diet, the huckleberry, elderberry, gooseberry, serviceberry, thimbleberries, chokecherries, and hawthorne berries. Those berries not eaten soon after being picked were pressed into cakes, dried and stored in baskets made from cedar roots and saved for the winter. Berries were often mixed with dried meat and made into pemmican or mixed with camas and kouse cakes to enhance the flavor of the biscuits.

With the coming of summer and the snow having melted from the mountains, the Indians traveled into the high country in search of the elk, the deer, the mountain sheep, and the bear. They needed the animals not only for meat, but also for their hides, with which to make clothing. The meat was dried and the hides tanned.

It was after the plateau Indians acquired the horse around the beginning of the eighteenth century that their way of life gradually evolved from an economy dependent on the salmon to a buffalo economy. The eastern plateau Indian, the Nez Perce, the Cayuse, and on occasion the Coeur d'Alene Indians traveled by horseback over the continental divide, to where they hunted the buffalo and soon adopted many of the ways of the plains Indian.

For the most part the pre-Columbian plateau Indian was well fed and enjoyed a life as free and unfettered as man has ever known in any society.

Chapter 8

Bad Medicine

Chief Winter Bull sat in his tipi brooding over the unfortunate circumstances which permitted the escape of the Long Knife. "His bow string had been broken." He was chagrined at the situation, but he had mixed emotions in his heart for he held much admiration for the mountain man because of his stamina and courage. The man had outrun every warrior in the tribe and had outwitted them all and left no sign as to his whereabouts in his escape.

But then all was not lost, for he held as a prisoner the beautiful Nez Perce wife of the Long Knife. Winter Bull was a strong chief, not only was he the war chief of the tribe, he was also the accepted leader in the governance of the tribe. He was twenty-six winters old and owned many horses and had two wives. He was, in the ways of the Blackfoot, a rich man and was looked on by the members of his tribe as a strong and just chief. But now his heart was troubled. He had come to desire the Nez Perce woman for she was the most desirable woman he had ever seen, but then his problem was that he already had two wives and to add another to his tipi would almost surely cause problems with his oldest wife. While polygamy was common among the people of his tribe, he was not sure that he wanted to incur the enmity of his first spouse, "She who sits by my side," although a second or third wife held the status of a servant or slave. But Winter Bull desired this young Nez Perce for his bed for she showed much spirit and he likened her to a young spring colt. He wanted to bed her down and take from her some of the haughtiness she exhibited. She was his captive and his slave and he could do with her as he wished. Where infidelity among the women was often treated with drastic action, often by cutting off the nose or ears of the wayward unchaste wife, the Blackfoot men took what they wanted pretty much as they wished. Winter Bull was chief and his actions would not be questioned. But then, there in the background was his older wife to contend with and she had borne him three fine sons, one of which would some day be chief of these Siksika, the Bow River Blackfeet. She had been a good wife for six years, although old and jaded before her time from hard work, and she was held in high esteem and satisfied his sexual desires as he needed her. But the consuming vision of Shining Moon kept pervading his thoughts and his burning desire for her soon overcame his reservations. He did not, however, count on the spirit of this Nez Perce woman, this fiercely proud daughter of a great Nez Perce chief who had chosen to spend her life as the wife of the Long Knife who had less than a year rescued her from these same hated Pahkees! Even though she was a prisoner and faced the chance of being killed, she stood her ground when approached by Winter Bull and refused his carnal advances. Although it was not apparent to others, she knew that she carried the child of the mountain man in her body. Even Josh did not know of this condition because it had been only in the last few weeks that Shining Moon had become aware of the fact. In her mind, she still had the hope that one day her husband would again rescue her from the Pahkees. She knew that as long as he was alive and she was a prisoner, Josh would be lurking in the vicinity patiently awaiting his chance to free her.

SHINING MOON'S PRAYER

O' guardian spirit who came to me with the wind
And on whom I now place my trust
Make my ears sharp
That I may listen for your voice
That will give me strength and wisdom
And guide me in a sacred manner
That I may search for and find
The man whose child now lives within my body.

As I gaze into the heavens at sunrise
As I did in my search for a guardian spirit
I again look for a sign

That will tell me that beyond the circle of tipis
There awaits the mountain man who will take me
    from the place.

O'Raven, hear my plea.
I see your strength for I am weak.

    The rebuff that Shining Moon gave the proud chief only whetted his appetite for her. Not only had he lost the chance to kill and scalp the Long Knife and thus inherit all of his great Medicine, but his manhood had been refused by this wilderness beauty. (The Blackfeet believed that the man who killed a great warrior would thereafter possess all of the prowess of the man he had killed.)

    Winter Bull was disconsolate. How could he regain the prestige that he felt he had lost. He sat in his tipi and brooded about this unenviable situation for two days. He could not decide on what action to take, so he entrusted his dilemma concerning Shining Moon to the medicine man, the shaman, of the tribe who was an old and wise warrior of the Blackfeet by the name of Swimming Bear, a man of many winters who had come to have some stature in the tribe because of his wisdom.

    Swimming Bear consulted with the spirits and as he was acting as an intermediary for the tribal chief, he spent several hours performing the rituals and incantations seeking the best possible solution to the problem. The advice he eventually gave Winter Bull was to divest himself of this woman, that he should travel alone to the far north and trade her to another Blackfoot tribe, that he had best never lay eyes on her again, as she was for him bad Medicine. He should do this as soon as possible, or at the latest before the moon was full or his medicine would not protect him on his journey if he tarried too long.

    On returning to his tipi, Winter Bull mulled over the advice of the shaman and decided that he should follow it. Besides, he could take along the pelts that he had stolen from the Long Knife and trade them to the King George men at Flathead Post for whiskey, powder, ball, and guns. He would ride north from his village through the pass into the valley of the Jocko and

Flathead Rivers and retrace his journey of the few days past when he had captured the woman. He was also anxious to ride the gray-spotted stallion that he had acquired. It was a horse of many gaits and he wanted to try it on the trail. The trip to the post would take two days on such a horse and he would leave early the next morning for he wished to rid himself of this woman and return to this village and prepare for the summer's wars.

The sky at dawn was filled with the high wispy clouds that foretold of a change in the weather. The wind worried the hair on the mane and whipped the tail of the prancing Appaloosa stallion, as Winter Bull and Shining Moon rode through the village followed by Midnight, the mule loaded with beaver pelts. Scrawny dogs scurried before the pair as they rode from the perimeter of the leather tipi village. The stallion was feisty and faunced at the bit in his mouth. What with this strange rider on his back, he would have given Winter Bull a difficult ride, except for the presence of Shining Moon nearby.

The pair rode at a fast gait to the northwest for about an hour and were approaching the pass, climbing steadily but not to any great elevation as they worked up to about 3,800 feet at the pass which was only 600 feet higher than the village. The surrounding mountains rose sharply before them, dominated by Squaw Peak at almost 8,000 feet elevation.

As the Blackfoot chief rode nearer to the pass, he became wary and watched for any unusual movements of animals or telltale reactions of the birds in the canyon. He listened intently and sniffed the shifting west wind and although he detected or saw nothing he felt was unusual, proceeded on into the canyon. He rode slowly, watching intently the trail ahead. He would have preferred to have had with him other warriors but he had followed the advice of the medicine man and had come alone. He felt somewhat better, however, when he remembered that Swimming Bear had said that the trip would be without incident if he did not tarry. Shining Moon, riding with hands tethered to the saddle horn and with her horse on a lead rope tied to Winter Bull's saddle was hopefully watching for some sign of her husband. It was then that she saw a Raven, her Wyakin, land in the top of a tree to the side of the trail and she wondered at the occurrence. "Her heart was good" for she now knew that somehow her Long Knife was near.

She knew that when the occasion presented itself that he would again try to rescue her from the Pahkee chief. As the three mounts approached a small stream crossing at a turn in the trail and they were preparing to descend into the stream bed, the attention of Winter Bull was diverted by the sudden movement of a tree to the left of the trail and he shifted his gaze from the stream bed in the direction of the disturbance. At the moment he looked away, he was unseated from his horse by the tremendous impact of a man's shoulder which struck him from behind to his right. As he was knocked to the ground, his gun, Josh's "Old Bullshooter," went flying from his grasp and landed clattering on the gravel. He was hit so hard that he was also separated from his Medicine bag. Both he and his

assailant landed on the ground along the stream bank, each grappling for a hand hold on the other. They both jumped to their feet facing each other. Winter Bull was somewhat dazed but intent on facing this unexpected danger. He saw before him an oddly clothed white man whom he soon identified as the escaped Long Knife who at the moment stood ready to launch himself at him. He also saw that the Long Knife was armed with a club made from a length of strong and supple alder wood. The chief took stock of his own position and knew that he needed a weapon for he had lost his rifle. He felt at his waist for his knife and found that, yes, it was there and jerked it from its sheath, just before he had to fend off a blow from the club wielded by the Long Knife. Thus the battle of position lasted for a minute or so but in the end the Blackfoot chief proved to be no match for the huge cat-like mountain man with his club, nor was he able to avoid the blows or to inflict any injury to his adversary. Finally, the tenacious young chief lay on the ground with his neck broken by a tremendous blow from the mountain man's club.

When the battle was over, Josh stood and looked at the body of the man who had been the reason for his torment during the past two weeks. Thinking that he had been a worthy adversary, however, he felt for him no remorse, as it had been a case of survival and it was good to regain once again all in life that was of consequence. But he would not scalp the body, for he himself had been given the chance to escape from capture by this strangely motivated latter-day errant knight. He would not deny him, as was the belief of the Indian, the chance to travel to the heights where he could view the land of the souls, the Happy Hunting Grounds, to ever hunt the buffalo and live on fat cow. Then Josh turned to his wife of such a few short months and drank in her beauty. How good it was to again have her with him. Josh could hardly believe his good fortune to have regained most of his worldly possessions, his horse, Midnight, the pack mule, the Hawken rifle, the Appaloosa stallion, the beaver pelts, and even his hand guns which he found in the Medicine bag of the dead chief. He had lost only his traps and his flute. He would not concern himself with their loss, however, for he must now travel fast from the land of the Blackfeet before the knowledge that their chief was missing became known to them. He would travel south up the Bitterroot River, over Lost Trail Pass of Lewis and Clark fame, and up the Salmon and Lemhi Rivers. From there, he would retrace much of the trail on which he had traveled north from the rendezvous that had been held on Henry's Fork of the Green River almost one year before. He would yet have time to make the rendezvous in Cache Valley that would be held during the last two weeks of May and into early June of the year 1826.

Eighth Interlude
Rocky Mountain Rendezvous — 1825-1840

The Rocky Mountain fur rendezvous was the brain child of General William H. Ashley. He, along with Major Andrew Henry, established the annual gathering as a means of supplying fur trappers with goods and accepting in trade the beaver hides brought in by the mountain men.

Some of the trappers who attended the rendezvous were company trappers, employees of the Ashley interests, but many were free trappers who hunted on their own but who attended the rendezvous and traded their furs to Ashley for supplies.

The site selected for holding a rendezvous was usually a high mountain valley where there was plenty of water and lots of green grass for horses to feed on, where the air was clear, and the temperature pleasing and the humidity low. Such a place was the valley of the Green River, the Siskadee — the prairie hen — along which seven of the sixteen rendezvous would take place.

Indians of many nations, the Nez Perce, Shoshone, Flathead, Eutah, and Bannock, also came to the rendezvous and were part of the scene. They came to trade their furs as well as engage in the yearly frolic.

There were sixteen identifiable rendezvous, the first having been held in 1825 and the last in 1840. While the concept of the trading fair was not unique to the fur trade, it was new to the Rocky Mountains and was instrumental in providing the impetus for one of the most colorful periods along the American frontier.

1825 — JULY 1 AND 2

The first Rocky Mountain rendezvous was held on Henry's Fork of the Green River, some 20 miles up the fork on the high ground between two streams, Birch Creek and Burnt Fork, near their confluence with the Henry's Fork of the Green

River. The location was an auspicious one for there was plenty of grass and water for the many horses and pack animals and lots of game in the vicinity. The rendezvous was attended by 120 men, 25 of whom had traveled west with General Ashley. There were very few Indians at this first rendezvous. Those who did attend were mostly ones who lived in the vicinity or were the wives of trappers. Ashley took back to St. Louis with him about 100 packs (100 pounds or about 66 pelts per pack) of beaver worth $50,000 which he had obtained in trade from his company trappers as well as the free trappers.

1826 — MAY 25 TO JULY 18 (the actual length is in question)

The second rendezvous was held in Cache Valley, a high mountain valley bordering the Bear River and straddling the modern-day border of Idaho and Utah. The valley is about twenty miles long and five miles wide, and is surrounded by high and rugged mountains, the Wasatch to the east and southeast and the Portneuf to the north and west. Ashley outfitted a supply caravan carrying merchandise worth $20,000. It was commanded by Jedediah Smith and Robert Campbell and was composed of 60 men and 160 pack mules. They headed west in late October of 1825 and were snowed in on the Republican River. General Ashley himself departed St. Louis on March 8, 1826 with 26 men. He caught up with Jed Smith and the supply caravan on April 1, 1826. Ashley sent Smith and Moses Harris on ahead to arrange the rendezvous in Cache Valley. The caravan arrived in the valley on May 25, 1826 and Ashley traded for 125 packs of pelts which were worth $60,000 in St. Louis. On July 18, 1826, Ashley sold the fur company to Jedediah Smith, David Jackson, and William Sublette (the SJS Company) for $16,000 to be paid for in beaver pelts at $3.00 a pound.

1827 — JULY 1 TO JULY 13

The 1827 rendezvous was held on the flat alluvial plain at the south end of Bear Lake, a lake that is about twenty miles long and eight miles wide and lies astride the border of modern-day Idaho and Utah. General Ashley had contracted with the Smith, Jackson, and Sublette fur company to transport supplies worth between $7,000 and $15,000 to the 1827 rendezvous, but actually transported supplies worth

$22,447.14. The supply caravan, composed of 46 men and commanded by James Bruffee and Hiram Scott, departed from St. Louis on April 12, 1827. It included a wheeled four-pound cannon, the first wheeled vehicle to cross the continental divide. The caravan arrived at the rendezvous site around the 1st day of July, 1827 and during the following two weeks traded with the trappers and Indians the supplies for 74 packs of beaver pelts, 95 pounds of castoreum, and 102 otter skins, all worth $33,270.72, which more than paid the debt owed to Ashley for the supplies as well as paying off a debt of $7,861 owed him and realized a profit on the year's trapping. The trappers came back to spend the long, hard winter in Cache Valley.

1828 — FIRST PART OF JULY

The fourth rendezvous was held, as had been the third, at the south end of Bear Lake. The supply caravan with $20,000 worth of supplies had been formed in St. Louis the previous fall by William Sublette and David Jackson, two of the SJS Fur Company partners and had traveled to the mountains, arriving in November. They traded the supplies for 77 packs of beaver pelts which William Sublette sold in St. Louis for $35,810.75 or a profit of nearly $16,000. Jed Smith, after exploration to California, spent the winter at the Hudson's Bay Company at Fort Vancouver on the Columbia River. After the rendezvous, David Jackson rode north to the vicinity of Flathead Lake in modern-day Montana.

1829 — JULY 1 TO 15 ON POPO AGIE AND AUGUST TO LATE SEPTEMBER AT PIERRE'S HOLE

There were two rendezvous held in 1829. The first of these took place in the valley where the Baldwin River and the North Fork meet to form the main stream of the Popo Agie River. William Sublette had spent the winter in St. Louis and departed the city with a caravan of 55 men and supplies worth $9,500.00. The supplies were traded for 45 packs of beaver for which the SJS Fur Company received $22,476 in St. Louis. Later in the summer, about 175 trappers assembled in Pierre's Hole for the second rendezvous of the year. Since the supplies had been distributed at the get-together held on the Popo Agie earlier in the summer, the Pierre's Hole gathering was apparently held for sports activities and for general rejoicing and camaraderie.

1830 — MIDDLE OF JULY

The location of the 1830 rendezvous was at the confluence of the Wind River and the Popo Agie River and near the modern-day town of Riverton, Wyoming, William Sublette, one of the SJS partners, brought supplies worth $30,000 to the rendezvous in 10 wagons and 2 dearborns (two-wheeled carts), the first wheeled vehicles, other than the cannon brought to the mountains in 1826, to travel what would be the eastern end of the Oregon Trail. SJS traded their supplies for 170 packs of beaver worth $84,499.14. The American Fur Company, once owned by John Jacob Astor, was now making itself felt in the Rocky Mountains. The SJS Fur Company sold out to the Rocky Mountain Fur Company of Henry Fraeb, Jean Gervais, Thomas Fitzpatrick, James Bridger, and Milton Sublette, for $15,532, due November 1, 1831.

1831

A rendezvous was not held in 1831. Thomas Fitzpatrick had arrived in St. Louis too late to meet with Sublette, Jackson, and Smith who had set off for Santa Fe earlier in the year. Fitzpatrick had no funds or credit available in St. Louis, so decided to follow SJS to Santa Fe and there obtain supplies. After obtaining $6,000 worth of material, he headed north toward the trapping grounds. Jedediah Smith was killed by Comanches on the Santa Fe Trail and Sublette and Jackson terminated their partnership. Some of the trappers assembled in Cache Valley and some went to the Green River, but a supply train did not arrive at either location.

1832 — JULY 8 TO 17

Occurring at Pierre's Hole in modern-day northeastern Idaho, the 1832 rendezvous was the largest ever held with over 1,000 trappers and Indians assembled. Attending the gathering were representatives and trappers from the Hudson's Bay Company, the American Fur Company, the Rocky Mountain Fur Company, several independent companies, and many free trappers. Because of the difficulty that Thomas Fitzpatrick of the Rocky Mountain Fur Company had encountered in obtaining funding for supplies, William Sublette contracted with the Rocky Mountain Fur Company to transport their supplies to the rendezvous of 1832. Sublette traded for 169 packs of beaver worth $58,305.75 at the rendezvous.

1833 — JULY 5 TO 18 (?)

The eighth rendezvous was held on the Green River. It probably started at Fort Bonneville but was moved to Horse Creek, five miles down the Green River from the fort. Supplies worth $15,000 were brought to the rendezvous by Robert Campbell and William Sublette who had formed the St. Louis Fur Company during the winter of 1832-33. Henry Fraeb of the Rocky Mountain Fur Company met Campbell and purchased the supplies. The combined companies in attendance at the meet sent 165 packs of beaver to St. Louis; the RMF Co., 62 packs; the St. Louis Fur Co., 30 packs; and Bonneville, 22½ packs.

1834 — JUNE 20 TO JULY 9

Rendezvous number nine was held on Hams Fork of the Green River. William Sublette transported supplies to the rendezvous and traded for 40 packs of beaver. Milton Sublette and Robert Campbell sold their holdings to the American Fur Company. John Jacob Astor sold the American Fur Company to Pratee, Chouteau and Co. of St. Louis. The Rocky Mountain Fur Company of Fraeb, Bridger, Gervais, Fitzpatrick, and Milton Sublette, was dissolved. Fitzpatrick formed a new company with partners Milton Sublette and James Bridger.

1835 — AUGUST 12 TO 21

This rendezvous was held in the same location along the Green River at Horse Creek as had been the 1833 gathering. Large numbers of Indians, Shoshone, Nez Perce, and Flathead, attended the rendezvous. Lucien Fontenelle of the American Fur Company transported supplies to the meet. Dr. Marcus Whitman, a missionary and also a medical doctor who established the mission near Walla Walla, Washington, traveled with the supply train. Fontenelle took 120 packs of beaver and 80 packs of buffalo robes back to St. Louis.

1836 — JULY 6

The 1836 rendezvous was held on Horse Creek as had been the 1833 and 1835 ones. Thomas Fitzpatrick of the American Fur Company transported the supplies to the rendezvous. Dr. Marcus Whitman and his wife, Narcissa, went west with the supply train. Also traveling with it were the Reverend and Mrs.

Henry H. Spalding who established the mission at Lapwai, Idaho. The American Fur Company effectively gained control of the fur trade in the Rocky Mountains, though it was declining as the silk hat replaced the felt hat among the gentry in the population centers of the world.

1837 — JULY 5 TO AUGUST 10

This meet was held twelve miles below Horse Creek at New Fork and included many whites and about three thousand Indians. Thomas Fitzpatrick brought supplies to the rendezvous and arrived there about July 5th. Jim Bridger was there with a suit of armor furnished by Sir William Drummond Stewart.

1838 — JUNE 23 TO JULY 12

The American Fur Company attempted to keep the place of the rendezvous a secret from the Hudson's Bay Company and it was held at the confluence of the Popo Agie and the Wind River near the oil spring. Hard times had hit the fur business and prices were low, about $3.00 a pelt and many trappers could not pay their debts incurred by high-priced supplies. Only about 20 packs of beaver were taken and 125 trappers attended the rendezvous. Trade was so unprofitable that there was doubt whether there would be a supply train in 1839.

1839 — JULY 5 TO 10

The rendezvous was held on the Green River again at Horse Creek. Pierre Chouteau sent a caravan of supplies to the rendezvous with Moses Harris in charge. The meeting was a quiet one with little drinking and frolicking. The Hudson's Bay Company sent a brigade to the rendezvous to keep alive the competition with the Americans.

1840 — JUNE 30 TO LATE JULY

The last rendezvous held in the Rocky Mountains took place on the Green River. An unusually large caravan with Andrew Drips in charge brought the supplies. With the caravan were also Jim Bridger and Henry Fraeb. Also with the caravan were Father Pierre Jean De Smet and the Reverends Harvey Clark, P.B. Littlejohn, and Alvin T. Smith and their wives. This last rendezvous brought to an end an era unlike any experienced before or since.

Chapter 9
Rendezvous 1826

Cache Valley straddles what would be in a later day the border between the states of Idaho and Utah. The valley is an ideal place to hold a fur rendezvous, as it is oblong, about five miles wide and twenty miles long. It is protected on all sides by high mountain ranges within which there are peaks rising up to 10,000 feet. The Wasatch Range to the east and south, the Portneuf Range to the north, and the Bannock Range to the west make up the mountain barriers. The elevation of the valley floor is almost a mile high, full of lush grass well suited for horse pasture with cool, clear streams for drinking water intersecting the valley in many places. The Bear River, the main stream through the valley, enters through a deep canyon to the north, winds along the west side below imposing Sedgwick Peak and flows out of the valley through another deep canyon to the west on its way to the Great Salt Lake. The many smaller streams which intersect the valley floor drain the water of the melting snow from the perpetual high mountain snow pack which lies on the glacial terraces of the precipitous north and east slopes of the higher peaks. There are streams named Gooseberry, Strawberry, Williams, Mink, Warm, Maple, Foster, Sugar, Flat, and Cub — streams that were full of beaver and otter, a mountain man's nirvana come true.

The valley and surrounding mountains afforded many kinds of game for food, including elk, deer, bear, mountain sheep, buffalo, and, of course, with such a concentration of wildlife, the predators, the cougar, bobcat, coyote, wolf, grizzly, and wolverine were also numerous. There were great flocks of waterfowl, geese, curlew, sandhill cranes, swans, and ducks. There were the grouse, the ruffed, blue, Franklin, sage and sharp-tailed. There were also fish, such as trout and whitefish in the streams. In the foothills were berries in season. To exist in such a place was possible almost without effort.

The mountain men found in these high mountain parks what the indigeous Indian had enjoyed for many centuries — a place as free and wild as man has ever seen. Throughout the West, the mountain man picked these natural parks, not only as the place to hold his fur rendezvous but also as a place for "winterin'." They would in years to come assemble in such places as Pierre's Hole, Jackson's Hole, Brown's Hole, Ogden's Hole, Burnt Hole, and several other such natural parks. These well-protected high mountain valleys afforded an easy living both in the summer as well as during the long cold winters. To the mountain man who every day faced a fearsome wilderness which he had to challenge just to stay alive, such places were a picnic, a salubrious setting for personal enjoyment and saturnalia.

The year previous, in 1825, what was considered to be the first Rocky Mountain fur rendezvous had been held on Henry's Fork of the Green River, located in the same relative geographical vicinity as would be the rendezvous of 1826. Henry's Fork of the Green River was about 80 miles as the crow flies to the east of Cache Valley, but from Cache Valley, it is difficult to reach by trail because of the high mountains which run north and south between the two valleys.

Twenty miles upstream from where Henry's Fork empties into the Green River is a small stream known as Burnt Fork. Here, too, the meadows are wide and covered with ample grass, food enough for the hundreds of horses ridden to the rendezvous by the mountain men, the traders, and the ever-present Indians.

The 1825 meeting was picturesque as would be all sixteen of the Rocky Mountain fur rendezvous. It was a wilderness fair — a fair where the mountain men brought from many parts of the West their hard-earned "hairy wampum," the harvest of the past year, their beaver plews to be offered in trade for supplies to sustain them for another year. They traded for hardware, guns, powder and ball, gun flints, knives, traps, and for tobacco, a pipeful of which helped pass the long, lonesome winter evenings. They traded for food to satisfy a latent but suppressed civilized desire for such luxuries as coffee, tea, sugar, salt, and flour — food which was not necessary for survival but which satisfied a cultivated, civilized taste that would never be lost, even after many winters in the wilderness. They traded also for "foofaraw," trinkets if you like, beads and bright-colored cloth, finger rings and earrings, sleighbells and hawkbells, ribbons, papers of vermilion, mirrors, needles and awls, buttons and fish hooks, all for their Indian wives, or if they had not married, for goods to trade in the future to some

comely Indian princess for the solace of the body.

The prices were high with sugar and coffee at $1.50 a pound, knives at $2.50 each, tobacco at $2.00 a pound, cloth at $6.00 a yard, but then in return, beaver skins brought a good price, $5.00 a plew.

For the goods that he had transported to the rendezvous on horse and mule back all the way from St. Louis, General William Ashley had taken home a sizeable profit for his ingenuity and efforts, about 9,000 pounds of beaver pelts worth $50,000 in St. Louis. Ashley also took back to that city an order for whiskey, an item that was noticeably missing at the first (1825) rendezvous. The mountain men thirsted something fierce for a drink of whiskey — whiskey that was usually made up of a little real whiskey, cut with branch water (plain water) to which was also added red pepper, cinnamon, and other spices to make it seem strong and hard to swallow, but which satisfied adequately that yearly thirst. Whiskey purchased at 15 cents a gallon and sold for as much as $4.00 a pint, a considerable profit. The rendezvous as a trading fair was not an Ashley original idea as the large trading companies had used such a fair as a get-together for their trappers for many years. However, such a meeting was unique to the Rocky Mountains.

What was different here was that many of the trappers were not employees of the company but came voluntarily to the rendezvous along with the employees of the company, there to replenish their depleted supplies and to enjoy the companionship of their kind. The long-established trading companies, such as the North West Company and the Hudson's Bay Company, usually operated from established trading posts and from these posts sent out brigades of hired trappers into the wilderness to catch beaver and other fur-bearing animals. The trappers in the brigades were usually voyageurs, "hommes du nord" and half-breed Indians, often Iroquois, recruited in Montreal or eastern Canada.

Ashley had reasoned correctly that if trappers would come to a trading fair, a rendezvous, each summer, he could make a sizeable profit, both on the trading goods which he transported to the rendezvous, marked up often as much as 2,000%, as well as clear a good profit on the furs, the beaver pelts which the mountain men traded for the high-priced supplies.

* * *

Josh Copeland and Shining Moon had arrived at Cache Valley, the location of the 1826 rendezvous, well ahead of the main body of trappers and a full week before the pack train loaded with supplies came in from St. Louis. But then, there was comfort in being once again in the company of other trappers, not only for the companionship, but also for the mutual protection from the marauding Blackfeet that was derived from superior numbers. Josh also needed a few days to recuperate from his narrow escape from the Blackfeet.

Shining Moon had made new clothing for Josh and herself as they had traveled to the rendezvous, clothing made from the skins of animals that Josh shot for food. While the clothing was not as good as that made from the leather of year-old tipi covering, it was adequate to protect them from the elements. Shining Moon was very adept at preparing leather into a usable product in a very short time. Upon their arrival in Cache Valley, Shining Moon had soon traded for some smoke-cured leather with the Shoshone Indians who were also assembled there for the rendezvous, and from this leather she soon prepared more suitable and durable clothing for Josh and herself.

Shining Moon also prepared medicine to soothe the pain and to heal the wounds that Josh had incurred in his ordeal in the Blackfoot gauntlet and his subsequent arduous but successful encounter with the wilderness. While many of the lesser wounds had healed, the pain of the numerous cankerous cactus spines in his feet persisted, had festered, and were squeezed out. To ease the pain, Shining Moon had collected the bark of the willow tree which Josh chewed and which deadened the pain. The bark contained salix — salicic acid — a drug that is one of nature's pain deadeners. Shining Moon also collected the sap of the balsam fir, which she applied to the wounds to hasten the healing. The turpentine in the blisters of the green balsam fir served effectively as a disinfectant. She also prepared a soothing salve made of balm of gilead tree buds. These were steeped in water and the liquid mixed with bear grease. It is probably that the bear grease was more beneficial than the bud broth for it kept the feverish skin soft and prevented it from cracking.

She also boiled the roots of old kouse plants — biscuit root — and used that broth as an insecticide. With these time-honored Indian remedies along with the rest and soaking of his body in the nearby hot springs, Josh soon was as healthy as ever.

Josh anxiously awaited the arrival of General Ashley and his supply train, for he anticipated the festivities as well as he wanted to trade his furs for much needed supplies and foofaraw for Shining Moon. The Blackfeet had taken from her all of the gifts he had bought her at Saleesh House and he wanted to replace them. Shining Moon was now showing evidence of pregnancy and although her weight had increased somewhat and she was noticeably awkward, she continued without difficulty to perform all of the camp chores necessary to keep her husband comfortable and well fed.

Shining Moon also tanned the hides of the buffalo that Josh shot for food and from them constructed a tipi, for she was looking forward to the day when there would be need for shelter for the child within her body, her first born, fathered by her mountain man husband.

Josh watched his wife in wonder and would lay his hand on her belly and feel the movement of the baby within and they together would laugh at the occasion in anticipation of the birth of the child which together the two of them had created.

* * *

General William H. Ashley had outfitted in St. Louis a supply train of one hundred horses and mules along with fifty men, each man riding a horse and leading a pack animal which was his responsibility for the entire trip. Ashley started up the Missouri River on March 8, 1826. He had followed it northwest to the Platte River, then up the Platte to the Sweetwater and Popo Agie rivers, over South Pass, and down to the Sandy Rivers, the Little and the Big, until he came to the Green River — the Sisk-ka-dee. He then traveled cross country southwest to the Bear River which he followed down to Cache Valley, arriving there in late June, 1826.

On his arrival at Cache Valley, Ashley found assembled there over two hundred trappers and several hundred Indians. The latter were mostly Shoshones, sometimes called Snake Indians because of the sinuous movement of their hands and fingers. About half of the white men assembled were free trappers and the remainder Ashley-Smith company trappers all of whom had traveled to the rendezvous from many parts of the West.

Those present included the likes of Jedediah Strong Smith, a company trapper who had replaced Major Andrew Henry as Ashley's partner at the 1825 rendezvous and who during the past year had taken a brigade of trappers west of the Great Salt Lake looking for the Buenaventura River. Campfire lore had it that the river ran to the western sea, but he found no such river. Neither did he find any beaver for the country was parched and dry and afforded few inhabitants, either critter or man.

Among the others present at the rendezvous were Etienne Provost who came to the rendezvous from Santa Fe with a brigade of trappers. There, too, was Jim Bridger from north along the Snake River who along with John Fitzgerald in 1823 had abandoned Hugh Glass to die from wounds inflicted on him when attacked by a grizzly bear. Glass, who had been left for dead, had recovered from the bloody ordeal and was able to make his way without any weapons, first by crawling and then by walking the two hundred and fifty miles to Fort Kiowa. It took him six long weeks of pain and suffering.

There, too, was Tom Fitzpatrick — Broken Hand — along with many other mountain men of stature, including Bill Sublette — old Cut Face. There, too, was David Jackson after whom Jackson's Hole was named and Jim Beckworth, a mulatto who told the tallest stories in the mountains and out of whose mouth tumbled lies as would the innards of a butchered buffler's stomach.

The mountain men as well as the Indians awaited with impatient expectation the arrival of the packtrain bearing the supplies needed for another year of trapping. There would also be whiskey to drink, and all, both red and white, would join in the celebration to release in one big "bust" the pent-up frustrations formed during the past year from the fears, sufferings, privations, dangers, sorrows, hardships, and disappointments. All of these were a part of the daily life of the mountain man, from which there was need for escape on occasion to keep one's sanity. The mountain man never knew when that arrow, that shot, accompanied by a gut-wrenching, savage yell might come from just beyond the perimeter of the flickering light of his campfire. Fortunately for the mountain man, the Indian was very superstitious, even to the point that he seldom attacked at night. This superstitious deterrent was so great that many Indians believed that to be killed at night committed the soul to wander the happy hunting ground in darkness through eternity.

Life for the mountain man was tenuous at best and when the occasion arose which permitted relaxation from the constant awareness of the hostile wilderness, he took advantage of it. He worked hard and he played with abandon.

Following the trading at which Josh acquired all the supplies he needed or desired as well, he joined in the games, the foot racing, the shooting contests, the wrestling, and the horse racing, but he drank little whiskey, unlike most of the others, for he had a family to care for. Josh won most of the contests in which he entered, for few men could best him in physical prowess and he was challenged by few and those who did had done so only after having drunk too much whiskey which had addled their minds. Josh's prize Appaloosa horse, Smoke, was by far the fastest horse at the rendezvous and with it won many races and also as many wagers. He was offered a year's wages for the fleet, sure-footed stallion but he refused all offers. In the Appaloosa horse, he owned what was probably the most dependable, most durable horse in the country. Such a horse under you could be the difference between life and death in a desperate situation.

Josh also enjoyed sitting around the campfire and swapping tales as much as did any man and offered his own version of many a hunt. For wherever the mountain men got together, there was much braggin' and yarnin'. When the trading was over, the whiskey all drunk up, and dallying with the Indian maidens had, temporarily at least, lost its attractiveness, the sporting events had been run — the running, the jumping, the racing, the wrestling, the fighting, the target shooting, and the horse riding, and when all the shouting and the dancing had subsided, the mountain men sat around the campfires and listened to the yarnin' by a monologuist — a talker who had a good sense of humor and who could keep the trappers enthralled with his tall tales. Such a man was Caleb Steel.

* * *

Caleb Steel was old and experienced by mountain man figgerin'. When to live in the mountains for seventeen years as he had without losing your top knot was no mean trick. Caleb was known to have said in his own words that "He was like an old buffler bull with one nut and one horn and all he could rightly do any more was crap and beller. But let me tell ya', he'd say, thar's lots of beaver lifts left in these old bones yet, waugh! Trappin' is fat doins' these days. Thar was a time back in the early 'teens when them varmit savages outnumbered us trappers a hundred to one. Ya made yer sets at dusk and lifted 'em before sun up and ya kept to the wormwood and willer brush during the day if ya wanted to keep ye'r topknot . . . eatin' cold jerky and squaw pemmican for breakfast and supper and maybe startin' a fire at mid-day when the breeze scattered what little smoke ya get from an aspen wood blaze.

"Yep, this niggur came west from St. Louie on a 60-foot keel boat up the Missouri River in the spring and summer of 1809 with Manuel Lisa, Major Alexander Henry, and a company of trappers . . . He's the same Henry who later jined up with General Ashley.

"Well, we traveled up that cursed river all summer, and with fall and winter comin' just over the horizon, we stopped that miserable boat at a village of Gros Ventres . . . Big Bellies . . . who lived along the Missouri near where it is jined by the Yellowstone River and we built a fort of cottonwood logs. In the spring, we moved on up the Missouri to where the three forks jined to form the big river. Thar we built another fort right in the middle of the Blackfeet country. Now ya talk about gettin' somewhere the hard way! Waugh! That hyar travelin' by keel boat is tougher than old buffler bull meat. This child'd sooner crawl on his shin bones all the way from St. Louie to South Pass than row, pole, push, and pull another keel boat up the Missouri again. That thar's one reason I ain't ever goin' back to St. Louie again. Waugh! In the spring that broilin' river is full of floatin' trees and bloated, stinkin' buffler carcasses that have fallen through the rotten ice during the spring. Why, the water is so muddy, it's too thick to drink but too thin to plow! In the evening, when yer camped, ya' dasen't wander too fer from camp to relieve yourself or you'd end up buzzard meat with yer scalp hangin' from the coup stick of some Ree (Arikara) brave. That is, till he could trade it for whiskey to the pork eaters from the Hudson's Bay Company.

Most nights, we anchored the boat on an island in the river if thar was one handy.

"Once ya got to where ya was a headin' and ya climbed off that monster of a boat, ya was livin' in shinin' times. There was plenty of tender buffler cow to eat. Waugh! Hump ribs and boudins puts any other eatin' fare in the shade! 'Cept it be roast beaver tail. No wonder them Indian squaws waxed fat with fixin's like that to eat all the time. But then, fat's the way for them to be fer it makes 'em warm in the winter an shade in the summer.

"Waugh! And, too, in them early days, the beaver was so thick a man spent all his time trappin' . . . either settin' or liftin' traps. A fellow was in the water so much he got all shriveled up like a dried persimmon . . . why thar was this hyar trapper that we all thought was a litter feller 'til come summer and he dried out and bejabbers if he wasn't bigger than most!

"Then, thar was the time back in '23 when me and Sam Varner was a pushin' north toward the lower reaches of the Popo Agie, fixin' to make some early fall beaver sets. Well along toward evening one day we came on fresh sign . . . about a half hour old . . . of what we took to be the pony tracks of a war party of about twelve Blackfoot warriors. They was travelin' north, slow like, toward the Wind River country.

"Now this child had no hankerin' for a fracas with any hostiles bent on addin' my topknot to the decorations on his coup stick, so I said to Sam, 'I'm a thinkin' we'd best ride up the middle fork of the Popo Agie for a spell 'til this hyar trail cools down a tad.' Old Sam agreed and we headed our bangtails west up the fork toward Wind River Peak which reared up thar in front of us to a tolerable height.

"We was a keepin' our eyes peeled for a hole to craw into 'til them varmints vamoosed from the country. The only likely cover we could find was some willers along the creek . . . for trees on the side hills from the Popo Agie to the Powder were as scarce as hair on a goose egg. The country lays in the downwind side of the Wind River Mountains which raise their hoary heads a couple miles up into the clouds and scrape out all the rain.

"Well, we holed up in a willer thicket and settled down to spend the rest of the day and be ready to slip away come dark. I ain't sure what tipped off them varmints . . . probably was old Sam's spoor, for he smelled worse than most. In comparison, he made an old mountain goat billy smell like a wild rose! In fact, the mosquitoes and no-see-ums had to be mighty hungry 'fore they would set down on him for a meal. When the rest of us would be slappin' bugs . . . they would be buzzin' around old Sam like bees around a bee tree.

"Well, them varmints came skulkin' up the ridges along about an hour before sundown lookin' for sign and keepin' away from cover. Them Blackfeet have a reputation for cussidness but they cherished their hides more'n most . . . their squaws blackened their faces, tore their hair, and carried on with a passel of wailin' when one of their own was sent to the happy huntin' grounds.

"Them Blackfeet kept their distance just beyond the range of his hyar long barreled flintlock. They know'd we was a hidin' somewhere in them willers but wasn't sure just where. We watched them from under a cut bank as they was a ridin' along the ridges above the draw tryin' to pick up a movement or catch the glint of the sun on a rifle . . . they rode up and down for a couple of miles, stoppin' now and then to palaver . . . squintin' into the low evenin' sun.

"Well, long toward dusk and they hadn't drawn a shot or flushed us from cover, some of the young bucks, itchin' for a scalp to hang on their coup sticks, begin ki-yi-ing and ridin' hard toward the thickest willers along the draw, actin' just like an old grizzly fresh out of hibernatin', chargin' the brush where a cow elk had hid her calf in 'em, hopin' to flush somethin'. But old Sam and me jest set ther 'tight as a buffler bull's bung in fly time' and let them itch. There was a time or two when old Sam wet the front sight of his smooth bore but he resisted the temptation to shoot and give our hidin' place away.

"Well, come twilight and they still hadn't figured out who we were or where we was hid, they rode down the ridge toward the Popo Agie, fixin' to make camp, and with a mind to makin' another try fer ha'r come sun-up. Well, this niggur had no intentions of bein'g in the invirons come daylight and saddled up just as soon as it was dark. Old Sam, though, was itchin' just like one of them thar dog soldiers lookin' for his first scalp. He was hankerin' to give them tipi creepers a taste of their own bile. He figured to put the fear of the old scratch in 'm for a bit. Now a dozen Blackfoot braves just ain't to be tampered with ... but when we saw by their campfire they was camped out in the open prairie, Sam 'lowed as how we should tie a log to a rope stretched between our horses, charge through their camp, and give a few of them a tumble that would have 'em huntin' through their medicine bags all winter lookin' for a charm. Waugh! What a ride ... we rode up close to the camp as quietly as we could and started our charge ... yellin' like a bunch of Comanches and tumbled the whole lot 'fore they knew what hit 'em. Why, they scattered like a covey of quail. This child and Sam laughed so hard at the look on them dog soldiers we almost split our buckskins. W'y we either put the fear of old scratch in 'em or they quit the country real quick for we never saw hide nor h'ar of them Injuns again.

* * *

"Then thar was the time when Butch Wilson decided to do some funnin' with some greenhorns who was just up the Missouri from St. Louie. Butch had a face for grinnin' and could no more pass up a chance for a funnin' than most could a good meal of buffler boudins. And he went to great lengths to arrange a funnin' situation.

"Butch had discovered in the hills near the fort a cave to which there were two openings and it gave him an idear for some fun. He talked a couple of them greenhorns into goin' huntin' with him to get some b'ar meat. The two did not know that they was to be the victims of a funnin' and they readily agreed to helping him to make meat, thinkin' he was serious. Well, Butch wandered around the hills fer a time with them tenderfeet in tow before it 'peared as how he had just chanced on to a cave. Butch stuck his head in the entrance and took a few sniffs of the air with his experienced nose and decided thar was a b'ar inside. So he told the two that he would go crawl inside and chase the b'ar out and they was to shoot it when it came by. Butch crawled into the cave with intentions of crawlin' out the second entrance and then high tailin' it back to the fort leavin' them two tenderfeet thar waitin' for the b'ar to come out and him sittin' back thar in the fort laughin' his heart out. Unbeknownst to Butch, Old Ephraim had just recently chosen that cave for hibernatin' and was all settled down in the cave for his winter's nap. As Butch crawled through the cave in the darkness, he crawled right up to that b'ar and bumped into him. Well, old Ephraim took a dim view of someone disturbing his sleep and let out a growl and took for Butch. Butch hit that b'ar across the nose with his flintlock and dazed him long enough for Butch to get away and he made a bee-line out of that cave with that critter right on his tail. Sure enough them two tenderfeet heard the growlin' and the runnin', and they shot that grizzly b'ar just as he cleared the mouth of the cave.

"Now Butch never let on as to what he was about, and them thar tenderfeet couldn't get over Butch's fearless courage and his beardin' that old grizzly b'ar right in his den. Little did they know that Butch's days of funnin' was over with that escapade for he figur'd that Mamma Wilson hadn't raised any fools and one such narrow excape was enough for him."

* * *

The campfire was burning lower, but Caleb took a long puff on his pipe and began again.

"Then thar was the time that a mountain man of considerable stature by the name of Gil Morey was bein' chased by a band of Blackfeet across the lava rock desert north of the Snake River and just south of the Lost River country. He had been ridin' hell bent southwest a couple days with them varmits after him in the witherin' heat of August without his comin' on any water fer himself or his mare. He was gettin' mighty thirsty and in need of water to wet his dry fer he had a spell back drained the last drop from his water bag.

"Late in the afternoon of the third day, with the hot bilin' sun still up thar three hands above the western horizon, Gil was pickin' his way through the belly-high sagebrush and the green and yellow lichen-covered black lava rock. He was leadin' his mare, tryin' to save her strength, fer he and the mare were both about done in and if he didn't find water soon, they'd both end up as buzzard meat.

"As he climbed to the top of a low black volcanic ash ridge and peer'd around him, lookin' fer any sign of them hostiles and seein' none, he looked for lines of willer or cottonwood trees which would tell him thar was water near. He couldn't see any trees but in the distance to the south, he thought he could see a lake of blue water a shimmerin' in the sunlight. It was sure invitin' to see. Waugh! What a sight! Now, thar would be fat doin's and he took new heart and headed south toward the lake. He traveled until sundown and the lake was still a fur piece away. Finally, with the comin' of darkness, he had to stop, fer travelin' through that rocky country in the dark was impossible. So Gil unsaddled and hobbled his mare and laid down exhausted under the sagebrush to sleep. His mouth and lips was all swelled up like a toad's so's he could hardly talk. His eyes itched and were red from the alkali dust and he felt he could go on no farther. He was so tired, though, that he slept that night and awoke with the dawn in spite of his misery. Gil felt somewhat better by morning and jumped up and looked for the lake but it wasn't there! But then, he thought it must be out thar somewhere fer he had seen it just before dark. Well, it finally soaked through his numbed brain that he had seen a mirage — the enigma of the desert which holds out before you what ya'd wanted so badly . . . a lake or a river . . . and now it was gone!

"Gil was hard put to know which way to go. He knew that to the south through the desert lay the Snake River but he was just as sure that without water fer him and his mare he wouldn't make it to the river. He turned and looked to the north to the range of mountains on the skyline but in his condition they was maybe two-three days away and probably beyond his reach and he figger'd them hostiles was headed in that direction as he hadn't seen hide nor har of them fer some time now.

"Gil finally decided to head south and try to cross a stream runnin' into the Snake River. He walked and stumbled through the desert all that day, still leadin' his mare and by mid afternoon, the heat of the sun beatin' down was more than he could endure, only his youth and strength, inured by weeks and months of physical privation, had carried him this fer. Now he was travelin' on guts alone as even the strength of this man could not last any longer. The sun and heat had taken thar toll and drained the last amount of energy from this totally exhausted mountain man. Thar had been no water for three days now and he didn't have the strength to overcome the need for moisture to replace that b'iled out by that blistern' sun. With evenin' comin' on and the sun droppin' ever so slowly toward the horizon, he came to a draw through some particularly rough ground and he knew he could go no farther and he dropped in his tracks and lay thar in a painful stupor almost wishin' that death would take him out of his painful misery. His mare stood head down, legs planted stiffly to either side almost over his body. How long he lay thar, he was not sure but a cool breath of air drifted down the draw and over the pain-wracked body of the mountain man and it slowly woke in him the desire to live. He slowly and painfully raised his head and saw through red-lidded and mattered eyes thar not fur from him was an opening in the lava rock around which the sagebrush grew larger than anywhere else and as wonder pierced and stimulated his mind, he tried to reason 'could thar be moisture in the cave'? He laid thar for a spell and then painfully crawled slowly toward the cave. Comin' from the mouth of the cave was a faint cool breeze and as he crawled inside he became aware of a strange blue light which seemed to come from within the cave. As he crawled farther into the cave, the air became colder and he wondered at the occurrence and then he saw a wall of ice and water drippin' from it. He was overcome with emotion for here was life-givin' water to quench his thirst. He laid down on his back and let the life-saving water drip into his mouth and run down his throat. After a period of time, the parched and swollen membranes in his mouth and throat were moistened and slowly shrunk and he was able to move his tongue and could swallow the delicious water. Then he rubbed the water over his face and around his neck and its coolness slowly brought him back to reality. He had stumbled into an ice cave in one of the volcanic lava tubes. This was almost unbelievable to find here in a parched dry desert — a cave in which ice had accumulated over the centuries. After he had consumed enough water to revive him, he filled his otter skin hat with the drippin' water and took it out to his mare who drank hungrily of the life-saving liquid. After a few such trips into the cave, both he and the mare were refreshed. Gil then ate some jerky fer the first time in four days and he felt much revived. Gil unsaddled and hobbled his mare and camped for the night and went to sleep listening to the mare contentedly cropp' the grass."

* * *

(Caleb got his second wind and continued)

"Now, a mountain man lived by his rifle and was always ready to brag about how fur it would shoot or how accurate it was and one such story went something like this:

"One day late in February old Wind River Billy was out ridin' his jenny lookin' for some fresh meat. The winter had been particularly long and hard and most of the game had drifted south. But thar was usually an old bull buffler hangin' around in the timber, if a feller kept an eye pealed fer one. On this particularly day, the wind was blowin' so hard that the tree squeaks were howlin'.

"In all that wind, Old Billy was having trouble gettin' fur from his cabin and knew he daren't go down wind or he'd never make it back before he'd starve to death. But he finally got up to the top of a rise not fur behind his cabin and looked around fer game. He hadn't looked long when downwind a mile or so he saw what looked like an old buffler bull hunched up in an Aspen grove. Well, not only was the bull too fur away, but he knew that it was a little crosswind, which would blow his bullet off course, so he tried to calculate how fur upwind he would need to shoot to carry to the old bull.

"Well, he got off his jenny and laid the old smoothbore over a log and took aim. The wind caught that bullet and sped it up and carried it downwind and hit that old buffler right between his eyes. Even though that was not a particularly good place to shoot an old buffler fer his head is pretty hard. But that ball had gained so much speed that it dropped that old bull right in his tracks. Now the problem was to get the bull butchered and back upwind to the cabin — and he would have never made it back against the wind if he hadn't been ridin' a pregnant jenny so that he had a way home."

Ninth Interlude

The Indian and the Buffalo

For the hunter, the buffalo hunt was one of extreme exhilaration, for to ride into the midst of a stampeding herd of buffalo, to know that if his horse stumbled or if an enraged bull decided to deviate from its headlong thoughtless flight and attempt to gore his horse with his short stubby horns propelled by a massive neck, meant almost sure death to the rider. The noise, the speed, and then the kill — such was an intoxicating and addicting event.

It took courage to ride into the stampeding, heaving, undulating, turning, twisting, swaying, snorting, grunting, bellowing, bawling, dusty, odoriferous mass — searching out, in the center of the herd, the most edible fat cows and two year old young buffalo. The moccasined feet of the rider touching the heaving side of the buffalo, giving your well-trained horse its head while the hunter nocked an arrow and drove it just behind the short ribs deep into the chest of the beast, searching for the heart, or if he missed the heart, piercing the lungs and killing by the longer method of hemorrhage, the hunter expending his arrows and then trying to work himself and horse out of the galloping mass through openings created by land forms and vegetation. And all the time galloping at the speed of the stampede and being constantly aware of that bull which would take you for an enemy and turn and lift your horse from the ground, unseat the rider who would be trampled into the dirt by the multitude! A few well coordinated and fortunate hunters had been known to jump from the back of one buffalo to another and thereby escape almost certain death. The hunt was no place for the faint-hearted.

A horse could overtake a buffalo at full gallop but it took a good horse to do so. The run was hard on horses and many soon became wind broken and were then of little use but for packing.

When there was buffalo to be killed, the men of the tribe would shoot in a day as many buffalo as the women could butcher and properly process the meat. For it was the women of the tribe who did the laborious work of skinning, cutting up, and hanging up the meat for drying. The meat of any buffalo not butchered on the day it was killed would sour and was then left for the wolf, the coyote, and the other scavengers that were always in evidence around the perimeter of a herd of buffalo.

The Indian women butchered a large buffalo by turning the carcass on its belly, extending its legs outward to either side to prop it up — a small animal might be butchered on its side — and cutting the hide down the center of the back, taking care not to sever the sinews in the back, sinews which would be split and used for sewing thread. All parts of the buffalo were utilized by the Indian, the meat, the sinews, the horns, the marrow bones, and the intestines — all for some purpose. The fat was boiled, refined, and stored in leather sacks for future use. The fat along the back was slowly sun- or fire-dried and cut into strips and eaten as "bread," a delicacy. The fat around the kidneys was eaten raw without drying or refining.

The freshly-butchered meat of the buffalo would be tossed into the spread-out hide and taken to camp where it would be processed in several ways. The first meat to be eaten was usually the tongue, for it was tender and easily taken from the animal and roasted. The taking of the tongue from the buffalo was a sacred ritual among many tribes. The parts of the buffalo that put all others in the shade were the boudins, the squeezed out intestines broiled by the fire and eaten in a long string. There were also the hump ribs, the hump and ribs from the back of the animal which were "willow sticked" — staked beside the fire and roasted, broiled. The Indians and the mountain men savored boudins and hump ribs and considered each a special delicacy.

The marrow bones, the back legs, were cracked and the marrow used as butter. It was often stored in the bladder of the buffalo. The horns were made into drinking cups. Some tribes spliced the ribs and made from them a short stiff bow. Other bones were used for digging tools, weapons, and pack saddles.

Buffalo meat was processed in several ways, but usually it was cut into thin strips or sheets, sun-dried or smoked and eaten as jerky. When dried, it could also be made into pemmican by pounding it into powder, a process which removed all of the gristle and sinew. The powdered meat was placed in parfleche bags in layers and melted fat poured over it. The bag was then tightly sewed up. The pemmican so prepared could be stored for years, was very nutritious, and could be eaten raw or cooked. Pemmican made into soup was known as "rubbaboo." When berries or other meats were available, many tribes made an excellent berry pemmican. Dried huckleberries, currants, elderberries, gooseberries, buffalo berries, chokecherries, and serviceberries were often used to spice up the meat. The huckleberry was considered to be the best of the berries because of the absence of seeds. Serviceberries and chokecherries contained large seeds but were used when other berries were not available. Almost any other kind of meat might be added to the buffalo meat — duck, grouse, goose — in making pemmican, thus adding to its flavor. Because it could be stored for long periods of time without spoiling, often for years, pemmican served as the staple to be eaten during the long cold winters, when game was hard to locate and fresh meat was almost unavailable. Pemmican also served as an excellent trail food, eaten when it was prudent to remain unseen and as quiet as possible when traveling through country known to be inhabited by hostiles. A handful of good berry pemmican made a good meal, regardless of the occasion, for it was as tasty as it was nutritious.

Then there was, of course, an undesirable product known by the trappers as "squaw pemmican" which was usually made from pounded, tough old buffalo bull that often as not contained maggots, flies, ants, and various other vermin to be eaten only when there was little else available.

In addition to cutting, hanging, and drying the meat, the women also had the difficult and time-consuming job of tanning the buffalo hides to be used as clothing and the many other items in the Indian's economy. Buffalo hides taken during the summer were usually tanned with the hair removed and made into tipi covers, moccasins, shields, saddle bags, canoe covers, parfleche trunks, rawhide thongs, and ropes. It was the winter hides taken when the hair was long and woolly that were tanned with the hair on and made into robes, winter clothing, bed robes, and winter moccasins.

To tan the hides, the women spent many long and difficult hours scraping and dressing the hides. The tanning of a buffalo hide was probably the most difficult work that the women engaged in and contributed much to the fact that an Indian woman was old by the time she was thirty.

The hides were stretched out and staked to the ground flesh up, wet down with water in which wood ashes had been mixed. This was the method used to remove the hair. They were then scraped with a sharp-edged instrument shaped like an adze. The tool was most often made from flint, elk horn, or buffalo bone. After being scraped — fleshed — the hides were wet down with a liquid made from buffalo brains. If time permitted, the skins were kept moist for about two weeks and each day they were draped over a tree limb or elevated log and pulled back and forth — kneaded — until they were soft and pliable. If the hides were to be used for clothing or for tipi covers, they were then smoked to help waterproof the leather. The tanned hides were then rolled up and stored for future use in making moccasins, mittens, leggings, shirts, and trousers.

If the hide was to be used for a shield, part of the hide from the shoulder of an old buffalo bull would be stretched over a frame and allowed to dry. The hide would dry so hard and tough that it would shed the bullet of a smoothbore fuzee, if the bullet did not strike the shield squarely.

* * *

Running with the buffalo was a most exciting and sporting way to hunt the animals. However, the Indians used several other methods of killing buffalo which included:

Still hunting: Where the hunter would disguise himself with the hide of a wolf or some other animal that was familiar to the buffalo and not cause him to take alarm and stampede. The hunter, covered by the hide, would crawl close enough to the herd to discharge an arrow. This method worked best in an area where the grass or sagebrush was tall enough to partially conceal the hunter. Hunting by stealth was the time honored way in which the Indian killed the buffalo before he acquired the horse or gun. This method, however, obviously was not as productive as were other methods.

The surround: This was accomplished by a group of horseback riders surrounding a small herd and the riders turning back into the herd any animals which attempted to break away. The buffalo would mill around and run into each other. It was then not too difficult to kill the animals with arrows or lances. This method was much safer than was running with the buffalo but did not work well with large herds.

The impoundment: This method was not often used because of the amount of work necessary to prepare the enclosure. Long feeder barriers made of brush and logs were built which led into a log enclosure which had a narrow opening. A herd of buffalo was located and stampeded toward the enclosure. The animals followed the brush fences into the enclosure from which they could not escape and were then killed with arrows and lances.

The jump: In that part of the country where a steep cliff was part of the terrain, the Indians would stampede a herd over the cliff and thereby kill most of the animals. There is such a place that was used for that purpose near where the three forks meet to form the Missouri River. The terrain leading to the fall is such that the buffalo do not anticipate a sheer drop-off and would blindly stampede over the fall to their death.

Chapter 10
The Buffalo Hunt

It was the dawning hour and the frosty-edged east wind sifted down the ridges and canyons of the mountains surrounding the Big Hole Valley. The now golden leaves of the aspen turned their backs on the cold early morning breeze of late September, each leaf making its last colorful stand before succumbing to the inevitable icy winds of autumn, then to lose its grip and drift downward to the ground, there to lay down a carpet of musty gold.

As the star-sprinkled quiet of night was shouldered aside by a building and ever-increasing cacophony of sounds . . . the madrigal call of the meadowlark announcing the dawn, the howling of a brace of furry coyote pups begging their mother for a meal, the bawling of the now robust and gamboling tawny buffalo calves searching through the multitude of shaggy beasts for their mothers, the several octave bugle of the mating bull elk establishing his territorial bounds within which he herded his harem of cows, and dominating all was the imposing gutteral and deep-throated bellowing of the rutting buffalo bulls, a sound that drifted across the valley and reverberated through the canyons of the bordering mountains. Each herd bull standing with head down, belligerently pawing the parched dry soil . . . raising clouds of dust . . . each challenging those precocious young bulls who would intrude on his family of cows. It was the fiercest and the strongest of bulls that would successfully defend or usurp from a weaker bull the right to father a generation of progeny and perpetuate nature's way of evolving an ever-improving generation of the species. All of these sounds combined to usher in yet another fall day in the western wilderness.

The combined Nez Perce and Flathead hunting camp was astir at the faintest light . . . Indian women bustling about untethering and saddling the fleetest buffalo horses, saddling

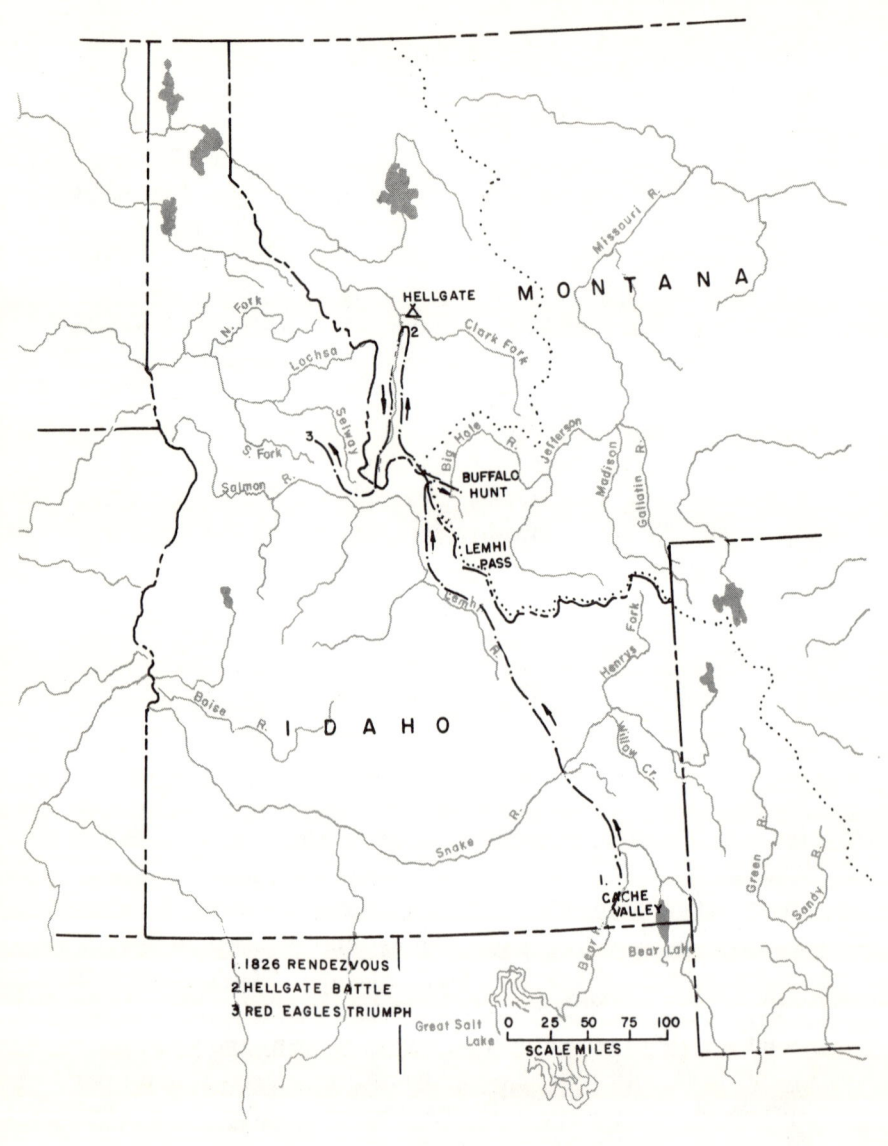

The Final Journey

their own pack horses, and sharpening their trade knives, all in preparation for the first big buffalo hunt of the fall, the success of which depended on how quickly and efficiently these same women could butcher and prepare the meat and hides.

The Nez Perce and Flatheads chose to hunt the buffalo during the moon of the first hard frosts when the days grow steadily shorter, yet still warm, and each successive night grew longer and colder. It was that time of the year when the furry backs of the buffalo quivered with each stiff-legged step . . . quivering from the accumulated fat gained during the long summer of eating the nutritious "grama grass," the short curly grass that grows close to the ground in much of the sparsely vegetated land of the West.

The Nez Perce and the Flatheads combined their camps and hunted the buffalo together to take advantage of their strength of numbers which together discouraged any attack by the Blackfeet who freely roamed the land east of the Bitterroot Mountains. The Blackfeet were opportunists and when they ascertained that a band of Indians were not able to adequately defend themselves or they thought they had the superior strength of numbers, they were always ready to acquire the horses, the personal possessions, and the women, children, and young as slaves from the unfortunate tribe. Men were never taken as prisoners except to be tortured and killed.

The tribe of Chief Black Elk had traveled east over the Nez Perce Trail to the Big Hole Valley, there to join up with tribes of Flatheads and other Nez Perce to hunt the buffalo. The Big Hole Valley was a favorite hunting area for the Nez Perce from Stites who usually spent the hot days of midsummer near the headwaters of the South Fork of the Kooskooski River and then early in the fall would travel over the Nez Perce Trail to the valley to hunt the buffalo before returning to their winter camp at Stites.

The Big Hole is a huge valley, forty miles long and fifteen miles wide, around which the horizon is interrupted at all points of the compass by high mountains . . . the Bitterroots to the west, the 9,000 foot high Pioneer Mountains to the east and south, and the Continental Divide to the north. The Big Hole is a high mountain valley not unlike the Cache Valley which is a ten-day horseback ride to the south, the site of the 1826 fur rendezvous. The Big Hole valley would, forty-one years later, be the location of one of the major battles of the Nez Perce Indian War.

Josh and Shining Moon arrived in the Big Hole in late September, anticipating and finding there the Nez Perce band of Chief Black Elk. They had traveled slowly through the high country that lay between Cache Valley and the Big Hole Valley enjoying the easy living and whenever possible giving the pregnant Shining Moon a modicum of rest.

The route taken by Josh and his wife from Cache Valley had been north up the Bear River to the place of the Soda Springs, here the Bear River skirts around the north end of the Wasatch Mountains and turns back south toward Bear Lake. The rugged and imposing Wasatch Range rises up in the thirty miles between Cache Valley and Bear Lake Valley. Bear Lake is about twenty-five miles long from north to south and about eight miles wide and straddles the Idaho-Utah border as does Cache Valley and would be the location of the 1827 fur rendezvous.

From Soda Springs, they had traveled north over the divide into the Snake River drainage and down Willow Creek to the Snake River, crossing it where it makes the big bend and turns to the southwest, thence north overland through the dry desert country of the sinks — where Birch Creek and the Big and Little Lost Rivers sink into the lava beds to run underground through the lava formations and emerge at the Thousand Springs, 150 miles to the southwest along the high, steep canyon walls of the Snake River.

While crossing the high but generally open level country that forms the divide between the Salmon and Snake River drainages, Josh had become aware that for two days a small band of Indians had been trailing him. He was not certain of their identity, but presumed them to be hostile and probably Blackfeet. Otherwise, they would have made themselves more visible. The open country through which they were traveling did not present a good place to set up an ambush and the Indians bided their time.

Late in the afternoon of an unusually warm day for September a sudden electrical storm closed over the pass and there was a deluge of water. Josh took this occasion to travel fast and hope that the rain would wash away his spoor. Such turned out to be the case for the rain fell for most of the night and he and Shining Moon evaded what was a small Blackfoot war party.

They had then continued unmolested down the Salmon River and up over Lost Trail Pass to the Big Hole Valley where they joined up with Chief Black Elk and his band. With their arrival, there was much happiness and rejoicing in the family of Black Elk, for it had been many moons since they had, early in the spring, departed from Stites for the fur rendezvous.

On the evening before the hunt, there was much ceremony, making of Medicine and smoking of the pipe. The Medicine Man of Black Elk's tribe, Gray Wolf, acknowledged by those assembled in the valley to have a reputation for making good Medicine, dressed up in his most festive costume, the skin of the gray wolf draped over his head and shoulders, and danced around the fire and appealed to the great spirit for a sign that now was the most auspicious time to hunt the buffalo. He stood in the smoke of the campfire and as it wreathed around his head, he looked up at the stars and tested the direction of the wind, reaching into his Medicine bag and withdrawing secret powders which he threw into the fire. After much dancing, supplicating, and the performing of incantations, he declared with gesticulations that the great spirit had revealed to him that with the sunrise the time was right to begin the hunt of the buffalo. There would be many buffalo and the hunters would shoot many animals of which the meat would be sweet and tender. For this approval by the great spirit, there was much joy and the throbbing of the tom-tom was heard well into the night and there was much dancing and frolicking throughout the camp.

* * *

It was the day of the hunt and just before dawn Josh along with the other men of the tribe, were preparing to run with the buffalo. Josh would ride his experienced buffalo horse, Smoke, the gift of Chief Black Elk. He would not use a bow and arrow but rather his two .65 caliber Ketland flintlock pistols. He would have two shots, one from each gun, and he would need to reload on the run. He practiced reloading the pistols and soon became proficient and could reload in about

20 seconds or about the same length of time it took an Indian to fire eight or ten arrows. However, in the middle of a herd of buffalo, the Indian could not maneuver his horse that quickly and Josh's disadvantage was not so significant. Josh shot and reloaded only one gun at a time for he kept the second pistol loaded just in case an enraged bull decided to turn and try to gore his horse and unseat him.

The scouts had been out since well before daylight and had returned with the information that a large herd of buffalo, estimated to be about a thousand head, were located generally in the middle of the Big Hole. This location was advantageous to the hunter as the lay of the land was relatively level and favorable for the run. They would kill what buffalo they could near the center of the valley, for in the north portion of the valley the Big Hole River divided into several channels which were bordered with willow bushes and the running with the buffalo would be more difficult in such terrain.

The men had prepared for many days for this hunt. They had made many arrows tipped with long, thin flint heads for piercing deep into the body of the buffalo, yet could be easily withdrawn from the carcass. The arrows were marked so that the person who shot the buffalo could be identified. The squaws made fun of the hunter who needed more than one or two arrows to down a buffalo. The bows were short and strong, the best of which were made from the horn of the mountain sheep. Bows made by the Nez Perce were eagerly sought in trade by Indians throughout the West and demanded a high trade value. Their bow strings were new and made from the sinew from the backs of these same buffalo. Their arrows were carried in a parfleche quiver which was slung on the Indian's back with the opening over the right shoulder. The bow and arrow was a weapon which was very effective in killing the buffalo and it seldom took more than one well-placed arrow to find the heart of a choice cow or two year old calf.

* * *

Ten sleeps had passed since the morning that Chief Winter Bull had ridden toward the standing star and as yet he had not returned from the journey. Neither had those who had recently traveled in that direction encountered him on the trail. People had become concerned and search parties were sent out to look for any sign of their chief and the Nez Perce woman. Only in that last day had any indication of his plight been discovered. Buzzards circled and the noisy ravens congregated near the entrance to the pass through the mountain range that separated the valleys of the Clark Fork and the Jacko Rivers and it was there that the unscalped body of their chief had been found, partly buried beneath a sand bar along the creek. The coyotes had just recently dug away the sand and partially exposed the body where Josh had hastily buried it in a shallow grave. The coyotes were scared away by the search party as they dug away the sand.

Consternation reigned in the Hellgate Blackfoot camp when it became known that the body of Chief Winter Bull had been found. There was much wailing by the women and their faces were blackened as a symbol of vengeance against those who had caused the death of their revered chief.

It did not take long for the three brothers of the chief to reconstruct the story of what had happened to their brother, for in the search of the vicinity, they found the blood-stained alder club that had served Josh as a weapon in his fight to regain his wife and precious possessions. They also found on the hill above the canyon the vantage point from which Josh had patiently set his vigil. They found also the twitch-up that Josh had rigged to attract the attention of Winter Bull. All of this evidence indicated to the brothers that it had been the escaped mountain man who had killed their brother. To confirm their suspicions was the fact that the body had not been scalped. An Indian would have scalped Chief Winter Bull and taken for himself all of the honors, the coups, and the deeds of the great Blackfoot chief. For to scalp the body was an act of annihilation and thereby the soul ceased to exist. If a warrior was killed and his scalp not taken, then he would in paradise be the servant of the warrior who had killed him.

There was vengeance to be taken and the three brothers of Winter Bull, all of whom were younger than the dead chief, ages eighteen, twenty, and twenty-three summers, all met together in solemn council. They consulted the Medicine Man, the shaman, and listened to his council. Each brother was a proven warrior with many coups and honors. Each had taken many scalps and any one of them was capable of succeeding Winter Bull as chief. But first there was the mountain man to be considered, his hair must be taken, his body mutilated, and he must be tortured and forced to show pain and fear! His scalp must be gotten and his soul annihilated and be forced to wander aimlessly through eternity, so to avenge the death of their brother.

The elders of the tribe met with the brothers in council to smoke the council pipe. The medicine man had prophesied after consultation with the great spirits that one of the three brothers of the chief should take the scalp of the mountain man in individual combat.

It was known by the Blackfeet that all of the "white eyes," the Boston Men, the Americans, had ridden toward Orion, the Hunter in the Sky, to the river that turned on itself and flowed from the direction of the standing star into the Great Salt Lake to trade their furs, that the chief of the trappers had traveled far from the land of the rising sun to the valley of the Bear River to trade supplies for the beaver pelts.

The Medicine Man counseled that the brothers of Chief Winter Bull should await the return of the mountain man to the Blackfoot country and then each in turn should seek out and kill him, if those who preceded each warrior had not been successful in his crusade of vengeance.

The body of the chief was wrapped in a green buffalo skin and placed in a cave, high in the mountains toward the rising sun near the Hellgate. The wives of the chief had wailed at his death, cutting off most of their hair and making huge gashes with knives in their arms, legs, and breasts.

With the coming of the moon of the first frosts, the elder brother, White Bear, felt that he should be the first to seek out the Long Knife and avenge the death of the chief and he began his preparation for this encounter with the mountain man. The message brought to the Blackfoot village at Hellgate by the wilderness telegraph was that a party of Blackfoot braves had seen whom they thought to be the huge mountain man and his wife traveling the high country between Birch Creek and the Lemhi River, but the wily Long Knife trapper had eluded them during a great lightning and rain storm which had swept through the mountains and erased his trail. It was known that the mountain man was traveling toward the Salmon River and probably would join up with the band of Nez Perce and Flathead Indians who were known to be camped in the Big Hole Valley preparing for their Fall buffalo hunt.

White Bear was a warrior who had taken many scalps. He had been a young dog soldier when he had procured his first Long Knife scalp. The unfortunate men were members of the Missouri Fur Company owned by Manuel Lisa who had ridden into the country where the three rivers join to form the big muddy, Missouri River, and he had taken the scalps of two of these trappers. The encounter occurred late one evening along the lower reaches of the Jefferson River when White Bear, along with a small war party, had chanced upon a beaver that had been just recently caught in a trap and was still struggling to keep its head above water, but was soon drowned by the weight of the trap. He reasoned that if he hid in the vicinity of the trap he would soon have a good chance to get his first Long Knife scalp. They waited through the night and just at daylight were aroused from fitful sleep by the movement of two white eyes in a canoe coming up the river toward the floating stick that marked the location of their catch. White Bear and his companions waited until the white eyes were abreast of their position and were working to get the particularly large beaver of over 80 pounds into the canoe. It was at that moment that White Bear chose to race his horse into the river, shooting arrows at the men, and in the melee the canoe was upset and the two trappers were captured. Their hands were bound with rawhide thongs and they were taken back to the Blackfoot camp where they were proudly paraded around the tipis. They were soon stripped of their clothes and the cruel blood-thirsty squaws stuck sharpened sticks into the unfortunate captives flesh just far enough that the wounds did not kill but caused great pain. One of the captives who had shown fear at the actions of the captors was strung up to an overhead limb. His body was stretched so that his toes just touched the ground and the squaws beat him unmercifully, forcing him to show pain and ask for mercy. He lost consciousness on several occasions during the ordeal and when he had regained consciousness for the fourth time and cried for mercy, the Blackfoot squaws cut him from throat to crotch and his bowels spilled out on the ground and he died screaming in agony, to be cut down and scalped by White Bear. All of this time, the second hunter who had shown no fear in his face and had stoically endured the pain had been spread-eagled and staked to the ground. He invisioned his fate as he listened to the laughter of the fiendish squaws at the last gasps and cries of his comrade. It seemed that the squaws had vented their spleen on the first trapper and did not bother the second, for in the sometimes enigmatic ways of the Indian, they went about their daily activities for the rest of the day. One Indian child even gave the trapper a drink of water. Through the evening and the long night, the trapper could only imagine his plight and the mosquitoes, buffalo flies, and no-see-ums feasted on his blood as he lay there quietly awaiting his fate.

With the coming of another day, the squaws prepared the trapper for their most gruesome torture. They cut off his eyelids, his lips, his nose, and his ears, buried him up to his neck in the sand and left him there in the sun to slowly die. The ants, yellow jackets, and flies, and soon maggots, crawled in and out of his wounds, which did not dry up for the squaws would walk by occasionally and beat on the exposed part of the head with sticks until he would begin bleeding again. It took him seven days to succumb from exposure and loss of blood. Through it all, however, the trapper made not one sound and acknowledged his fate stoically. Mercifully, he was unconscious from pain most of the time.

It was three days after the news that the huge Long Knife had returned to the country of the Hellgate Blackfeet that White Bear started his preparation, and began his fast to cleanse his body and soul to please his guardian spirit.

He also sat in a sweat house and then immersed his body in the cold water of the Clark Fork River after he had sweated profusely. He drank quantities of fish oil and pushed flexible willow withes down his throat to induce vomiting.

He smoked the ceremonial pipe with the elders of the tribe and listened to their haranguing. He sought the advice of the Medicine Man and got from him certain amulets which he included in his Medicine bag. These amulets, along with the pinches of colored sand, were part of his secret Medicine. He also wrapped hair of the white bear, the silver-tip grizzly, in the leaves of the devil's club plant as part of his Medicine.

He painted his face and arms for war and also painted his favorite war horse, a white and brown pinto, with appropriate designs — the animal's neck and chest with red and yellow geometric figures, the rump with black and red lines, and he tied feather streamers to the tail and mane.

When in his mind he felt he was ready to accomplish his mission, he rode his pinto war horse through the village shouting war cries and crying vengeance on the mountain man. He struck the post in the center of the village with his coup stick and rode out of the camp to the south, up the valley of the Bitterroot River toward the Big Hole Valley, on his solitary quest to seek out this man and bring back his scalp, if not his body.

White Bear rode to the Big Hole and from a concealed vantage point in the foothills bordering the valley watched the Nez Perce as they prepared to run with the buffalo. He watched as the buffalo hunters rode out to either side of the herd and stampeded the animals to the north, the hunters riding into the middle of the herd and shooting the fat cows with arrows. He watched also as the women rode out in the wake of the stampede to butcher the fallen buffalo.

White Bear followed north with the stampede, keeping to the timber and behind the hills out of sight of the hunters, always watching for the mountain man whom he hoped was among the hunters.

As the fury of the hunt diminished and the sun approached its zenith in the sky, White Bear neared Joseph Creek when he observed a rider veer from the herd and ride after a cow that appeared to be wounded and was running toward the trees that bordered the valley. It was then that White Bear recognized the rider as a white man, the Long Knife that was the focal point of his quest.

* * *

As the stampeding herd of buffalo thundered by a canyon formed by Joseph Creek, a young fat cow that Josh had just shot with his pistol, although mortally wounded, had not been felled by the shot. It continued to run, veering to the west toward a stand of thinly-spaced ponderosa pine trees. Josh chose to follow after the wounded cow to shoot her again and he turned out of the heaving mass of stampeding animals to follow it.

Josh caught up with the cow just as it reached the edge of the timber and discharged into it a bullet from his second pistol, for in his effort to catch the cow he had not taken time to reload his first pistol. The second shot killed the cow and Josh dismounted from his horse to give it a chance to blow. He and the other hunters had already killed as many buffalo as could be taken care of by the women and his horse was winded and needed a rest. Just as he dismounted, another horseman, an Indian, rode swiftly across the narrow valley and up into the trees where Josh stood by the fallen buffalo. Josh saw at a glance that the Indian was a Blackfoot and was painted for war.

White Bear brought his horse to a sliding halt and jumped to the ground facing Josh and made signs that he was there on a personal mission to avenge the death of his brother, Chief Winter Bull, and even if he were not successful in his mission, his two brothers, Many Coups or Two Antelope would follow him. In the eyes of his assailant, Josh could see the reflection of centuries of man's survival in the wilderness. It was the look of a man who feared no other man and who held no compassion, a man willing to give his own life to achieve a vengeful purpose.

Curiously, this son of the wilderness was to exhibit a code of honor as would a knight errant. His Medicine was so strong that he did not shoot his intended victim from ambush, neither did he intend to kill him by treachery. He confronted his adversary directly and by sign gave the mountain man a choice of weapons. It would be, Josh knew, a fight to the death with his only weapon, a knife.

Although tired from the long run with the buffalo, Josh was aware of his predicament and took his knife from its sheath and prepared to defend himself from this threat to his life.

The two men circled each other, each seeking an opening to attack, each feinting and hoping to cause his opponent to lose his balance and thus gain an advantage, giving him the chance to strike the killing blow.

Josh soon found that his was a fight for his life more difficult than any he had ever before experienced. This man, although considerably smaller in stature, was his equal in quickness and ability and Josh's attempts to strike him with his knife or to feint him out of position seemed to be fruitless. Josh could feel his strength diminishing as the heat of the hot mid-day sun bore down on his head and the sweat streamed in enervating rivulets down his face and dripped from his nose and chin and his breath came in increasingly shorter gasps.

Josh reasoned that he must wear down his opponent by imposing in some way his superior strength on this wilderness Spartan and he closed on his opponent, taking the chance of his being wounded, and the two fell to the ground, each grasping the knife hand of the other. It was after a fierce struggle during which the superior weight and strength of the mountain man proved to be the difference in the battle that Josh forced his knife into the heart of the courageous Blackfoot brave.

Josh was by this time exhausted and stood over the dead body of his opponent wondering at the persistance of these people, these sons of the wilderness who knew survival only by the strength of one's body and who had the ability to mentally inure themselves so as to have complete disregard for their own well-being. His was a civilization based on a code of personal courage that was usually lost to man when he became more sophisticated and his surroundings became less dangerous and he was not personally required to defend himself to survive but rather depended on others hired by the group to protect him from those who would infringe on his person. Josh chose not to scalp the body of his adversary in this his greatest test for his life. Although he did not hold with the beliefs of these people, he did respect them and refrained from prejudicing their ideas. He only had admiration for a man who, against long odds which, although known, were disregarded. It had been a personal fight, one of an eye for an eye, and one in which this wilderness man of honor had given his life.

* * *

The moon waned from full to new, a span of time that certainly was adequate for White Bear to have traveled to the Big Hole Valley and taken the mountain man's scalp, avenging the death of his brother, and to have returned victorious with the scalp tied to his coup stick. Such had not been the case, however. Many Coups, a warrior more renowned and celebrated in the Hellgate Blackfoot tribe than was his older brother, now felt obligated to take the trail in search of the trapper or to make contact with White Bear, for possibly the search for the white man had not been successful.

Many Coups performed the ceremonial rights to cleanse his soul and to appease the great spirit, prepared his Medicine, and painted his body and his horse in preparation for his quest. On a clear frosty morning early in the moon of the first snows, he headed his prized war pony up the Bitterroot River in the same direction as had his older brother. He would determine whether the Nez Perce were still encamped in the Big Hole Valley or had completed their hunt and were on the trail back to their winter camp. Examination of the trail at Lost Trail Pass told Many Coups that there had not been any appreciable recent movement over the pass and that the Nez Perce were still encamped in the Big Hole Valley, still in the process of drying the recently killed buffalo meat and tanning the hides.

Many Coups debated as to whether he should descend into the valley and search out the mountain man or to await him as he traveled the trail toward the winter camp. He was, however, in no mood to defer his confrontation with the mountain man and urged his horse along the trail down Joseph Creek into the Big Hole. Many Coups was armed with a fusee, a trade smooth-bore flintlock rifle, a knife, and a bow made from the wood of the osage orange and flint tipped arrows of service berry wood. He also carried a coup stick from which hung several scalps. He, like his brother White Bear, would confront the white man and search in his eyes for any evidence of fear to satisfy for himself the nature of this man before he killed him by whatever weapon was most appropriate at the moment.

On reaching the foothills of the mountains above the valley floor, he rode to the edge of a neck of timber and watched the movement in the valley and soon located the combined Nez Perce-Flathead hunting camp. They were, he saw, camped about three miles toward the center of the valley and next to the river. It would be difficult for him to approach the camp without detection, for there was no appreciable cover except a few willow bushes along some of the creeks.

He waited until late afternoon to approach the camp, a time when the sinking sun was low in the west, just above the mountains, making it a little more difficult for anyone to detect movement in his direction. He also followed what cover was afforded by willow trees along a small tributary of the Big Hole River running toward the hunting camp. He wanted to get a better view of the camp and possibly see the mountain man or to locate his living quarters in the camp. He rode undetected to within a half mile of the camp and there, behind a slight rise, he dismounted, tied his horse in the willows, and crawled to the top of the rise. He watched for some time the movements in the camp and could see that some of the people were preparing to break camp. Sheets of buffalo meat that had been hung on racks to dry had for the most part, been taken down and stored in parfleche trunks. The hides that would have been staked out on the ground were almost all taken up. The herders were moving the horses closer to camp. The camp had the look of one that would soon be moved.

Many Coups reasoned that unless he encountered the mountain man on this day, he would have difficulty locating him individually during the trek over the Nez Perce Trail back to winter camp.

The sun dropped behind the Bitterroot Mountains to the southwest and the smoke of the evening campfires spread out over the valley on the quiet, almost windless, evening. Many Coups located what he thought was the tipi of the mountain man next to what he presumed to be the tipi of Chief Black Elk, for outside the tipi was tied the gray Appaloosa buffalo horse that Many Coups recognized as the one that his brother Winter Bull had taken from the Long Knife when he had been a captive at Hellgate Camp.

Many Coups decided to wait until darkness and slip into camp and try to catch the trapper as he slept, kill, and scalp him. While a night attack was contrary to the Medicine of Many Coups, he must seek the life of the white man at all costs.

* * *

Two weeks had elapsed since Josh had vanquished White Bear in the fight for his life. The meat of the buffalo that had been killed in the hunt had been jerked and dried for the winter's food. The hides had been laboriously tanned, worked by the women until they were in condition to roll and take along to winter camp where they would be further tanned and made into useful articles.

With each successive night, the constellation of Orion, The Hunter, rose higher in the southern sky. The nights grew steadily colder in the valley of the Big Hole River. The termination dust, the snow, crept ever lower down the sides of the high mountain peaks surrounding the valley. The stark, now leafless gray limbs of the aspen protruded nakedly into the graying fall sky, for the north wind had stripped them of their gilded adornment.

Trumpeter swans, Canada geese, sandhill cranes, and many species of ducks at times almost darkened the sky as they winged their noisy way southward to spend the winter in the swamps and bayous of the warm southland.

It was time for the tribe of Chief Black Elk to return to winter camp on the Kooskooski. There had been in the tipi of the chief a little reluctance to start the trek because of the imminent birth of a child, that of Josh and Shining Moon. Shining Moon had for two days now shown signs of impending delivery. But the trip could be postponed no longer as any day now the heavens could drop enough snow on the high country to make the trip over the trail very difficult.

The following day was selected as the time to start the trip. The signs were right, the buffalo meat had been dried and packed into the parfleche trunks in preparation for travel. The hides had been rolled and on the following morning, the tipis would be struck and the trip begun.

With the arrival of evening, Shining Moon knew that her time to have her child had come for she was experiencing ever increasing contractions of her body. The sun was just dropping below the western sky and it was apparent that her time was at hand. Josh chose this time to leave the tipi and mounted his horse and rode slowly outside camp toward the setting sun thinking of the impending birth, wondering whether the child would be a boy to whom he could teach the ways and secrets of the wilderness, or would the child be a girl that could in days to come help Shining Moon in her daily chores. He would prefer very much that the child be a boy, but whichever it was he would love and protect it.

As Josh topped a small rise in the valley floor about a half mile from camp, he was aware of a quietness which made him alert to his surroundings. He had been preoccupied with the impending birth and was too late to recognize danger before he heard the whisper and almost immediately the shock of an arrow as it struck him in the back of his shoulder. He dropped to the ground on the off side of his horse, looking about as he did for his unknown assailant. The pain from the heavy flint arrow head slicing deeply into his shoulder and glancing off the bone made him sick and he winced as he dropped hard to the ground.

Josh swallowed hard and breathed deeply to choke back the wave of pain that welled over him and his body threatened to lapse into unconsciousness to ease the pain, an escape from which Josh knew he would never awaken.

The victorious battle cry of the Blackfoot brave Many Coups rang loudly in his ears and even though the pain in his shoulder was almost unbearable, Josh heaved his body up to meet the on-rushing charge of the warrior whom he saw through pain-blurred vision bearing down on him. Unbelievably, the Indian had in his hand a coup stick with which he was about to touch this hated mountain man.

Josh had had the presence of mind to hold onto his rifle even though the shock of the arrow had numbed for a moment the fingers of his left hand.

Josh brought up his Hawken at point blank range and pulled the trigger. Many Coups saw the movement and jumped aside but not before the bullet tore through his right arm. He was spun around from the shock of the half ounce of lead and dropped to the ground. He immediately jumped to his feet, however, grasping with his good left arm for his knife with which he would end the life of this mountain man. The battle was over quickly, however, as the adrenalin that pumped into Josh's body had cleared his mind and he withdrew his knife from its sheath and plunged it into the body of Many Coups. Feeling no remorse, Josh looked at the prostrate savage before him, then reached down and tore the scalp from his head.

Josh climbed on his horse which had stood nearby all this time busily cropping grass and rode back to camp to find that he was the father of a new young warrior.

Black Elk broke off the arrow shaft and pushed it on through the flesh of Josh's shoulder. The arrow had glanced off the bone and had gone almost completely through the shoulder. A poultice of bear grease and balsam pitch was applied to the wound.

Josh related the story of the attacks that had been made on him by White Bear and Many Coups to Chief Black Elk and to Shining Moon and that White Bear had told him that yet another brother of Winter Bull, Two Antelope, would seek his life if either the other two brothers were unsuccessful. It would be several days before Josh would have full use of his left arm and he chose not to expose himself to the attack that he knew would ultimately come from Two Antelope.

Chief Black Elk considered the attacks on Josh by the Pahkees and decided to call a council of war with the chiefs of the Flatheads and the other Nez Perce bands. The chiefs assembled and Black Elk addressed the council:

"My chiefs, hear me now. Our enemies, the Pahkees, have invaded our midst with warriors who would take the life of the Long Knife, father of my grandson. They have twice captured and held prisoner my daughter of the moon and only as a result of the bravery of the Long Knife has she survived. Now they have vowed to take the life of our white brother and have already sent two of their bravest warriors to avenge what they say is the death of their departed chief.

"We are many and as never before could settle many of the old scores heaped on our people and correct many of the indignities that we have suffered for so many moons. However, we must think first of the safety of our women and children, but then we can travel with them into the redoubts of the high mountains along the Nez Perce trail and there fortify a position where only a few men can easily protect them. Then our warriors who are five hundred strong, as many as there are birds in the sky, can ride the trail down the Bitterroot River and there avenge the indignities we have suffered for so many years.

"In past summers, our guns have been few and the Pahkees had many for the King George men of the Hudson's Bay Company have supplied them well for many years. Now that the Boston men from beyond the rising sun have come into the land to trap the beaver, we too now have many guns.

"Now is the time to avenge the loss of many of our brave

sons. We must bring fear to the eyes of the Pahkees and see their faces turn the color of the snow. We want to see them cry for mercy. We must bring to their knees these people who have treated our people as does the buffalo for the ant. It has been our wish to be at peace and we would bury the tomahawk, but our enemies are serpents with forked tongues. They give us no choice and we must take up our weapons.

"Let us paint our faces and string our bows and erase from the land this scourge which for so many seasons have been a thorn in our feet."

* * *

After the speech by Black Elk, the members of the council talked well into the night and each chief in his turn told of the many scalps he had taken and of the many wounds he had incurred in wars with the Pahkees.

It was the decision of the chiefs' council that the path to war would be taken to avenge past indignities placed on them by the Blackfeet.

When the chiefs had disbanded and gone back to their tribes, there was much activity in the combined camps and the throbbing of many tom-toms was heard. The warriors painted their faces and prepared their strongest medicine for the coming foray. There were war dances in the camps and the ever-increasing sound of the dances filled the night.

The assemblage of Nez Perce and Flathead peoples in the combined hunting camps constituted a considerable fighting force for there were over five hundred warriors but also to be considered was that with the group were all of the women and children as well as their winter's supply of meat. An attack on the Pahkee camp would mean the loss of many lives. Also, they would need to split their forces to protect their families and their food supply. They would take the women and children and the food supply to the redoubts of the high country along the Nez Perce Trail where with only a few warriors they could defend with ease their belongings. The majority of the warriors could then return to the valley of the Bitterroot and attack the camp of the Blackfeet.

Tenth Interlude
Significant Events in the Development of Trapping in the Northwestern United States

1670   The Hudson's Bay Company was chartered by King Charles II, giving it "the sole trade and commerce of all those seas, streightes, bayes, rivers, lakes, creekes, and soundes in whatever latitude they may be, that lye within the entrance of the streightes, commonly called Hudsons streights."

1787   Captain Robert Gray of Boston, Massachusetts sailed to the northwest coast to trade with the Indians for furs. He and John Kendrick had sailed in two ships — the *Lady Washington* and the *Columbia* respectively — Gray traded ships with Kendrick along the northwest coast and circumnavigated the world, the first vessel of American registry to do so.

1775-88   North West Fur Company formed in Montreal, Quebec with Britishers Joseph Frobisher, Benjamin Frobisher, Simon McTavish, Peter Pond, Alexander Mackenzie, David Thompson, and Simon Fraser as partners. To Peter Pond goes much of the credit for the early exploration into western Canada.

1789   Alexander Mackenzie of the North West Company reached Great Slave Lake and traveled down the Mackenzie River to the Arctic Ocean.

1792   Captain Robert Gray returned to the North Pacific where he discovered and sailed up the Columbia River.

1793   Alexander Mackenzie reached the Pacific Ocean at the mouth of the Bella Coola River in present British Columbia. Mackenzie wrote a book "Voyages from Montreal, on the River St. Laurence, through the Continent of North America, to the Frozen and Pacific

Ocean: in the Years 1789 and 1793," which President Thomas Jefferson read and which played some part in Jefferson's sending the Lewis and Clark expedition to the Pacific Ocean.

1801-02 Fifteen ships of several countries traded for 15,000 sea otter skins with the Indians living along the northwest American coast.

1803 The United States purchased the Louisiana Territory from France.

1804-06 President Thomas Jefferson commissioned Captains Meriwether Lewis and William Clark to lead an expedition to the Pacific Ocean by way of the Missouri River to the Rocky Mountains, across the continental divide and down the Columbia River.

1806 Between August 3 and 20, Lewis and Clark met eleven separate parties of fur trappers as they descended the Missouri River on their return from the Pacific Ocean.

1806 John Coulter, a member of the Lewis and Clark expedition, joined with Joseph Dickson and Forrest Handcock who were headed up the Missouri River to the Rocky Mountains to trap beaver.

1807 David Thompson of the North West Company built Kootenae House on Lake Windermere on the headwaters of the Columbia River.

1807 Manuel Lisa, William Morrison, Pierre Menard all fur company partners from St. Louis sent an expedition of fur trappers up the Missouri River. The expedition was commanded by George Drouillard who had been a member of the Lewis and Clark expedition.

1807-08 Lisa established Fort Lisa at the mouth of the Yellowstone River on the Missouri River and they wintered there.

1808 David Thompson of the North West Company established Kootenai House (2nd) on the Clark Fork River near present day Libby, Montana. It consisted only of leather lodges.

1809   The Missouri Fur Company, a combine of St. Louis merchants Lisa, Menard, Morrison, Pierre Chouteau, William Clark, Reuben Lewis (brother of Meriwether) and Andrew Henry sent 13 keelboats and 350 men upriver to trap.

1809   David Thompson built Saleesh House near Thompson Falls on the Clark Fork River (a tributary of the Columbia River). He wintered there in 1809-10. In the spring of 1809 he built Kullyspell House on Lake Pend O'Reille, near Hope, Idaho.

1810   Jaco Finlay and Finan McDonald of the North West Company built Spokane House near the confluence of the Little Spokane River and the Spokane River.

1810-11   Andrew Henry of the Missouri Fur Company traveled up the Missouri River to the vicinity of Three Forks, Montana and from there over the continental divide to present day St. Anthony, Idaho on Henry's Fork of the Snake River, where he built Ft. Henry and wintered. In the spring he moved to the Big Horn River and down the Missouri, arriving in St. Louis in the fall.

1810   (September) J.J. Astor's Pacific Fur Company, a subsidiary of the American Fur Company, commissioned a two prong fur trading expedition to the northwest Pacific Coast. The ship "Tonquin" captained by Jonathan Thorn, set sail on 8 September 1810 to establish Ft. Astoria, near the mouth of the Columbia River. They arrived there on 22 March 1811. A party led by William Price Hunt was to travel overland to Ft. Astoria. The party departed St. Louis on 12 March 1811.

1811   William Price Hunt and party, which included Donald McKenzie, Ramsay Crooks, Robert McClelland, Joseph Miller, and others, traveled up the Missouri as far as the Arikara villages near the present North and South Dakota line where they traded their boats to Manuel Lisa for horses and proceeded overland to Fort Astoria, arriving there in January 1812.

1812 (August) Donald McKenzie of the Pacific Fur Company established a trading post on the north side of the Clearwater River opposite the present day town of Lewiston, Idaho.

1813 The United States war of 1812 with Great Britain forced the sale of Astoria to the North West Company on October 6, 1813 (renamed Fort George) for $58,291.02, a considerable loss to the Pacific Fur Company.

1818 The Treaty of Ghent returned to United States all territorial conquests by England in the War of 1812. Ft. Astoria was returned to the Pacific Fur Company. The treaty also decreed that the Oregon Country be jointly occupied by the United States and Great Britain.

1821 The North West Company merged with the Hudson's Bay Company and the H.B.C. moved out of the Hudson's Bay drainage and took over fur operations in northwestern United States. (March 26, 1821). The new charter was liberalized on July 2, 1821 and permission was given to conduct a fur trade westward to the "Stony Mountains."

1822 Joshua Pilcher of the Missouri Fur Company had 300 men trading and trapping on the Missouri River.

1822 William Henry Ashley was joined by Andrew Henry and they built Fort Henry at the mouth of the Yellowstone River.

1823 Henry traveled up the Yellowstone River and built another Fort Henry. He sent trappers into the mountains. Jedediah Smith, one of Ashley's lieutenants, and party departed Ft. Kiowa and joined John Weber, another of Ashley's lieutenants at winter camp.

1824 The Hudson's Bay Company established Fort Vancouver at Belle Vue Point on the north side of the Columbia River opposite the mouth of the Willamette River. The construction was supervised by Dr. John McLoughlin and George Simpson.

1824 Jed Smith and trappers traveled up the Sweetwater River over South Pass and down to the Green River. In the fall Smith went with the British to Flathead Post (Saleesh House) on the Clark Fork River. Thomas Fitzpatrick and James Clyman, two of Ashley's men, took the year's catch of furs down the Missouri River to St. Louis with news of rich beaver country. Ashley led a pack horse supply train up the Platte River in November.

1824 (December 20) Peter Skene Ogden of the Hudson's Bay Company departed Flathead Post on the Clark Fork River and with a party of 75 men traveled into the Snake and Salmon Rivers and as far south as Great Salt Lake. His party caught 3,090 beaver. Jed Smith came with him.

1825 Ashley reached the Green River in April 1825 and there divided his men into trapping parties with instructions for all to meet for the 1st Rocky Mountain rendezvous on Henry's Fork of Green River in July.

1826 Ashley sold the fur company to Jedediah Smith, David Jackson, and William Sublette.

1828 The American Fur Company which had been formed by John J. Astor in 1808 now moved back into the Rocky Mountain fur trade. Lucien Fontenelle, Henry Vanderburgh, Andrew Drips, and Charles Bent brought trade goods and trappers.

1830 The Rocky Mountain Fur Company was formed by Tom Fitzpatrick, James Bridger, Milton G. Sublette, Henry Fraeb, and Jean Baptiste Gervais. They purchased the S-J-S Company from Smith, Jackson, and Sublette.

1840 Year of the last rendezvous in the Rocky Mountains and was held on the Green River and brought to an end an era unlike any before or since.

1846 International Boundary established along the 49th parallel between the United States and Canada.

Chapter 11

The Battle

In the camp of the Siksika, the Hellgate Blackfeet, there was turmoil and consternation. It was early morning, an hour after daylight and the scouts had brought back to the camp the information that a large force of warriors, Nez Perce and Flatheads, were approaching down the Bitterroot Valley. The dust raised from the many hundreds of horses could be seen in the early morning light as they passed through the narrows of the river, five miles to the south.

The Hellgate tribe was without a chief of record for none had been so designated since the death of Chief Winter Bull. Neither of the two brothers of the chief, White Bear or Many Coups, had returned to the village with the scalp of the mountain man. There was no time now to select a chief, but as in all emergencies there is usually one who assumes command and such was the case in this situation. The third brother, the youngest brother of Chief Winter Bull, Two Antelope, mounted his roan stallion and rode through the camp shouting epithets, proclaiming the Nez Perce and the Flatheads to be eaters of dogs and fish and that they would be driven from the land. The Flathead nation had been annihilated and driven deep into the mountains many years ago by the bravery of the Siksika. Now who were they to challenge the sovereignty of the Siksika? They would be driven back into their holes in the mountains with their tails tucked between their legs.

The people rallied behind this self-proclaimed leader, Two Antelope, and prepared to meet this threat. They would brush away these intruders on the land as one would step on a locust.

Little did the Blackfeet realize that the Nez Perce and Flatheads were now armed almost to the man with muzzle-loading trade guns which they had acquired from the American trappers. The ensuing battle would not be as one-sided in fire power as had been the case for many seasons since the days that the Siksika invaded this land from the Bow River in Canada, when they were the only tribes who had many guns — guns that had been supplied to them by the traders of the Hudson's Bay Company. With their superior fire power, the Siksika had pushed the Flatheads out of their traditional tribal lands in the headwaters of the Missouri and Clark Fork Rivers. They had also displaced the Shoshone and even the Crow Indians, none of whom then had guns in any number. For a generation, the Siksika had held dominion over the land from the Musselshell to the Bitterroot Mountains and almost without opposition rode rough-shod over the land, even as far as the Bear River far to the south.

They, the Siksika — the Blackfoot nation — were 60,000 strong, an aggressive people who had carved from the wilderness an empire that would ultimately fall only to the scourge of the white man's diseases. The great exterminators of the Indian who had no natural immunity were measles, smallpox, and cholera.

The Hellgate Blackfoot village of 60 lodges was located on the north side of the Clark Fork River and to the west of the confluence of Rattlesnake Creek with the Clark Fork and only a short ride from the narrows in the latter river, the Hellgate, a narrow canyon that could be easily defended.

Two Antelope sent the women and children into the high country above the Hellgate. He then dispersed along the shallows of the Clark Fork one-fourth of his warriors, men who knew the tactics of battle better than most Indian tribes, with the possible exception of the enemy who now confronted them. He would defend his village with these men dug in among the willows and cottonwoods. He knew that the enemy would try to overrun and pillage the village. The Blackfeet were a wealthy tribe for they had for many years demanded and received tribute from the less fortunate Indians in the upper Missouri Valley.

Two Antelope sent another sixty warriors into the Hellgate, there to be in position when he drew the enemy into the trap he intended to spring. He divided the other half of his men into two mounted patrols of cavalry. One of these he himself would command and with which he would cross the Clark Fork and ride out to meet the enemy, to seek to palaver with them and tell them that they should give up this ridiculous battle, for they would be defeated and many brave warriors would be killed. Their women would tear their hair and slash their arms and breasts. The Siksika were invincible and could not be defeated in battle.

The other remaining mounted force Two Antelope sent into the wooded hills to the north behind the village to be held in reserve if it appeared that the enemy would break through the prepared defenses and cross the river.

Two Antelope would, if the enemy persisted, fall back across the Clark Fork through his defense line of foxholes along the river bank and stop the enemy at the river. If this failed to stop them, he would decoy them into the narrows, the Hellgate, and there from superior high ground positions annihilate them.

* * *

The combined forces of the Nez Perce and Flatheads, almost 400 strong, rode down the Bitterroot Valley toward the Blackfoot camp. They had located their women and children in the steep country near Thunder Mountain in a region so rugged that the few warriors who remained there could easily defend the trail if necessary.

While the combined attacking force would operate generally as one, each tribe was led by its own war chief. Black Elk of the Stites Nez Perce was, however, acknowledged as the chief of chiefs.

During the night and before the war party arrived in the vicinity of the Hellgate village, Josh was given the command of fifty Nez Perce warriors from the village of Black Elk. He was familiar with the terrain around the Blackfoot village and with his warriors would cross the Clark Fork about three miles down river from the camp and near the mouth of the Bitterroot River. The purpose of this command was to attack from behind the warriors defending the village whom they reasoned would be guarding the village along the banks of the river. While the main Nez Perce-Flathead force was launching a frontal attack on the Blackfeet aligned along the river, the diversionary force would attempt to encircle the defenders and catch them in a cross fire.

Another force of about 100 mounted warriors under the command of Crooked Horn, a famous Flathead war chief, was to travel through the foothills to the east of the Bitterroot Valley and cross the Clark Fork between the Hellgate valley and the narrows. They could in this way cut off a retreat by the village defenders into the narrows. The main body of 250 mounted warriors would launch a frontal attack on the Blackfoot warriors defending the village.

As the formidable legions of Nez Perce and Flathead warriors approached to just beyond smooth-bore musket range (100 yards), Two Antelope and his mounted force of sixty of the finest Blackfoot warriors aligned themselves between the enemy and the Clark Fork River. Such a confrontation had not been commonplace in the recent history of the Hellgate Siksikai, for seldom had the Nez Perce and the Flatheads combined to fight them. Even on this occasion, the foray was an afterthought as the primary purpose of the alliance had been for hunting the buffalo to obtain meat and hides for sustenance during the winter to come. It was only after the two brothers of Winter Bull had attempted to take the life of Josh Copeland, Chief Black Elk's son-in-law, had the two groups of Indians decided to use their combined strength to teach the Pahkees a lesson in warfare.

The legions of gaily painted warriors which reined their mounts to a halt on the field of battle facing each other were in no particular military order, but each was roughly aligned behind the particular war chief to whom they had declared allegiance. The feathers on the coup sticks and the headdresses of each warrior fluttered in the early morning east wind. The dust that had been raised by the onrushing legions now drifted to the west and was dispersed by the breeze. At this moment, there was little sound save the snorting and stamping of the gaily painted war ponies and the ever-present buzzing of bald-faced hornets and yellow jackets.

The tenor of the moment was fraught with anticipation, each warrior had made his amends with his own personal god, his Wyakin, and had on the evening before sorted through the contents of his medicine bag and arranged each item in its place on the ground before him and prepared himself to exhibit the ultimate in bravery. Each warrior preferred to engage his adversary in hand to hand combat and even though he would discharge his fusee at the enemy, there would be little time to reload his weapon as he dashed headlong into battle. It would be with the arrow, the knife, and the tomahawk that each individual warrior would count coup and take the scalp of the enemy.

Each warrior had mixed the paint and applied it to his face and body in the designs that gave him strength to vanquish the enemy. If he were killed in battle, such a death was considered to be the epitome of bravery and because of this honor, the warrior took many unnecessary risks and demonstrated unusual actions. The warrior would often be caught up in his religious fervor and display complete disregard for his own livelihood so as to exhibit to his fellow warriors his bravery. To count a coup, to touch an enemy with a coup stick, even in the face of certain death, was not unusual.

Before a battle, it was traditional for the adversaries to first hesitate and palaver. In this case, the unlikely aggressor, the Nez Perce and Flatheads, hesitated before the Pahkees while Chief Black Elk and six lesser chiefs rode forward to meet the two emissaries of the Siksika, Two Antelope and a war chief by the name of Bear Tooth.

Chief Black Elk, astride a magnificent white Appaloosa stallion marked with a spotted black blanket which covered its hind quarters, rode slowly with reserved dignity to meet the Siksika. The chief cast his golden eagle feathered lance into the dusty parched earth before the Siksika and spoke:

"The heart of the Chopunnish are heavy for they came to the Big Hole Valley from over the Bitterroot Mountains in peace toward the rising sun to hunt the buffalo. For from the buffalo they get meat to fill the bellies and hides to warm the bodies of the old people and the children during the long cold winters. But the Pahkees have been treacherous and sent two assassins into the Chopunnish camp to take the life of the Long Knife who is the father of the newborn Chopunnish chief.

"The Chopunnish are weary of being harassed in their hunting and trading by the Pahkees. The Pahkees have shown that they are poor neighbors and should be shown that the Chopunnish too have the strength to coerce others if they chose to do so. Many seasons ago, the Flatheads were driven from their ancestral lands by the Pahkees and they now seek revenge for this transgression. They and the Chopunnish have combined their forces and will sweep the Pahkees from the land as does the wind that carries away the dust from the feet of the horses.

"Go and tell your squaws to begin their wailing and to prepare the burial gowns for your time on this earth is short. Your spirits will soon travel to the spirit world to meet those of your ancestors.

"The Chopunnish and the Flatheads will soon leave the field of battle the victor with many scalps and honors. They will count coups and avenge the many wrongs that the Pahkees have dealt the Chopunnish and Flatheads for so many seasons."

Two Antelope, the self-proclaimed chief of the Siksika now voiced his disdain for the threats of Chief Black Elk and he spoke:

"The Siksika do not hear the threats of those who are to us no greater than are the yellow jackets who buzz around the horse dung. Even Kipitaki, the old woman in the moon, would not believe that the Chopunnish and the Flatheads could defeat the Siksika in battle. The sweet water in the stream will turn sour on the day that anyone defeats the Siksika in battle. Turn your horses around and tuck your tails between your legs as would a whipped puppy dog and return to your squaws or before this day is over the Siksika will dance the scalp dance with your scalps in a hoop at the end of a pole and be paraded through the village. We will defeat you in battle and then seek out your women and children and make them slaves of the Siksika. Let us now see who only blows himself up as does the toad to frighten his enemies. Turn your horses around or fight as does the Siksika."

With that threat, Two Antelope and Bear Tooth turned their horses about and rejoined their legions of warriors.

At a signal from Chief Black Elk, the silence that had pervaded the battlefield was now rent with an ever-increasing cacophy of sound . . . the thundering of hundreds of horses hooves pounding the hard dry ground, the shrill battle cry of many soon-to-die warriors, each bent on demonstrating his bravery not only to his companions but also to the enemy in exhibiting the almost insane religion of bravado, the firing of the trade gun at the enemy at a distance of 100 yards — a distance at which anyone who was hit was just unlucky, the whine of the richochetting bullet skipping off the rocky river bank, the squealing of the horses hit by bullets or arrows, the sounds of their bowels as they galloped, the twang of the bow strings, the almost soundless flight of the arrow, and the thud as it struck a warrior or a horse.

Added to this tumult was the clashing of parfleche-covered, heraldic-painted war shields when struck by a tomahawk as when the opponents closed on one another and engaged in hand to hand fighting, and then the splashing of the Siksika horses as they retreated back across the Clark Fork riverbank defense lines, followed closely by the now victory-sensing legions of Nez Perce and Flathead warriors, many of whom were to fall to the guns of the dug-in defense forces.

But then from the west down the river and behind them came the legions led by Josh Copeland and whose cross fire negated the advantage of the dug-in Siksika forces who at the onslaught of the frontal attack and the pressure from the flank forced the withdrawal of the command of Two Antelope which now mounted their horses and fled toward the safety of the

Hellgate with the intent of drawing the enemy into the trap he had set but whom themselves had to fight their way through the forces of Chief Crooked Horn before they could reach the safety of the canyon. In the fight, many Siksika made the supreme sacrifice and achieved their immortal quest of dying in battle. Two Antelope was one of those who did not escape into the Hellgate and died at the hand of a Flathead warrior whom he had long oppressed.

But though the day had been won by the Nez Perce and the Flatheads, Chief Black Elk had no intention of following the Siksika into the trap. They would be content with the honors they had already won and the booty they would find in the abandoned village.

For the dead, there would be no memorials for the nomad builds none. But there would be anguish and wailing by the relatives and by the professional wailers for both the victors and the vanquished. The scalps of the defeated would be trimmed and hooped and would serve as the center of attention at the scalp dance in the victor's camp. There had been many examples of bravery. Many warriors had counted coup and many would boast of their bravery during the remainder of their lives and recount the story of how the Chopunnish and the Flatheads had beaten and avenged the many indignities and past defeats by the Pahkees. History would not record who won this battle for its participants had no written language. Only the tongue of the old people would tell the young of its happening.

Eleventh Interlude
Medicine

The facets of his life that were important to the plateau Indian were: his personal Medicine, his honor, and his status among his fellow warriors, and to count coup, to display physical prowess in battle, and to endure pain. To accomplish these purposes, the Indian often exhibited actions which were extreme. The preparatory rites to many of these actions were often as bizarre as the actions themselves.

To make Medicine was to go through an often elaborate preparatory ritual. The purpose of making Medicine was to enlist aid from his personal gods in the quest, trip, or battle on which he was about to launch himself, so to fortify his confidence and to make him invincible, to exhort himself into a psychological fever much like the modern day athlete "psyches" himself or herself "up" for the game or sports event in which he or she is about to participate. If the action in which the Indian was to participate involved several members of the band, such as being a member of a war party, the party might engage in a dance during which they would exhort themselves into a frenzy during which some members might exhaust themselves to the point of losing consciousness. The Indian carried in his Medicine bundle or bag items which were befitting to the superstition of that particular Indian not unlike our finding a four-leaf clover or carrying a rabbit's foot for good luck. Included in the contents of the Medicine bag might be bits of bone of the particular animal or bird with which he could identify. There were also feathers, bits of hide, swatches of hair, bits of reptiles, and sand of different colors.

The individual would often take sweat baths and purge himself by drinking fish oil. He might force willow withes down his throat to induce vomiting and thus purify himself in the face of his gods and thus enhance his chance for success on the mission he was about to undertake.

As the Indian put great faith in the good Medicine that came from smoking the pipe, he had a pipe for every occasion, and one of the most important parts of preparation that must be engaged in was to sit down with those involved to smoke the pipe.

The painting of both themselves and their horses was also important to the Indians in the making of Medicine and although each individual painted himself and his horse with designs which could be identified with the individual, there were certain patterns and designs which were more or less universal among the band or tribe. Just as the modern day woman paints herself to supposedly enhance her beauty, so did the Indian women use colored earth and where available "vermilion" on her face.

Probably one of the most bizarre behaviors exhibited by the Indian was that of "counting coup," an action in which the person would run or ride up to an enemy and touch him with a coup stick, even though in doing so the Indian endangered his life. That, of course, was the reason for the action for it demonstrated extreme bravery and total disregard for death or injury. To exhibit such bravery was very honorable and to live through such an act brought many accolades from his fellow warriors. There would be many stories about the event told around the council fires. To count coup and to endure pain without any facial or outward expression is not particularly difficult to rationalize as life itself in the environment in which the Indian lived was dangerous and to live to an old age was unusual.

To wage war provided a place for the warrior to exhibit physical prowess and to count coup. To die in battle was very honorable and enhanced his chance of entry into the Happy Hunting Grounds, a place where he would always eat "fat buffalo cow" and have the best horses and weapons. If he was fortunate and killed a particularly brave warrior in battle he would not scalp that enemy for by doing so he believed that the enemy would forever be his servant in the hereafter.

The Indian feared death by strangulation for he believed that the soul escapes from the body through the mouth. So it was that he did not wish to die by hanging.

The Indian also believed that to be scalped annihilated the soul and thereby it ceased to exist and there would be no life after death. While we consider many of the actions of the Indians to be odd, I am sure that many of the things that modern-day man does without a second thought would seem just as odd to the plateau Indian.

Chapter 12
Vengeance Is Mine

Red Eagle had long been bent on satisfying the gnawing grievance to his pride — of removing from his mind this festering thorn in his life, the mountain man, Josh Copeland.

The refusal by Shining Moon of his offer of marriage had been a personal defeat he could not handle. It was difficult for a fledgling dog soldier, the son of the famous war chief Cut Nose to establish a reputation during a time when his village was at peace with their neighbors. All summer long Red Eagle had sought guidance in his life from his Wyakin, the golden eagle, but thoughts of redress for his wounded pride had permeated and poisoned his thoughts as well as his disposition. The three older brothers of Red Eagle had taunted him incessantly about his rebuff, and he had sought solace in the silence of the wilderness. During the late summer, he had spent many days in the high country, searching out the white bear, the grizzly, hoping to wreak vengeance on this most feared animal of the wilderness. His weapon was only the bow and arrow and he intended to kill and take home the claws and teeth of this fearsome denizen of the wilds. If he could single-handedly subdue a white bear, he would regain to some degree his confidence and his stature with his family and fellow warriors. Status to a Nez Perce warrior was of primary importance. There was nothing in the life of a young dog soldier of greater importance than his reputation among his fellow warriors.

Red Eagle had hunted diligently but unsuccessfully for the white bear well into the late months of summer but had been unable to kill one. The white bear, old Ephraim, the grizzly, was not uncommon in these parts, but he ranged widely through the territory and was often difficult to find, let alone kill without endangering one's own life.

By the moon of the bugling of the bull elk, Red Eagle had

not as yet satisfied his consuming rage and he still seethed with vengeance upon his return to his village. So it was that when the word arrived on the Potlatch River that the Long Knife, the source of Red Eagle's misery, was back in Kooskooski country, Red Eagle was elated. While spending the many days through the summer and fall hunting vainly for the white bear, Red Eagle had decided that he would search out the Long Knife and take his life. Red Eagle turned over and over in his mind a plan of how best to kill the trapper and regain his stature in the Nez Perce village. He dreamed day and night of how he would hang on his lance the scalp of the white man. He reasoned that killing the man would be easy. He would follow him into the mountains and kill him while he was occupied in setting his traps to catch taxtspolya'ya the beaver.

Red Eagle spent the next two days engaged in performing purification rites. He fasted, drank fish oil as a physic, and forced flexible willow withes down his throat so to remove by vomiting all the fluids from his stomach.

He then set about assembling the contents of his Medicine bag. He felt that he needed the head and feathers of a golden eagle to satisfy his need for "medicine." To fulfill this want, he traveled up the Kooskooski River to the place of the shoulders of prismatic basalt which terraced the steep almost vertical mountain side. It was here on the rock bluffs high above the valley of the river that the golden eagle nested. In the meadow below the bluffs, Red Eagle dug a pit which was large enough for him to sit in comfortably. He covered the pit with the straight limbs of the serviceberry bush which he interlaced so that they would hold up the weight of a snowshoe hare, the bait with which he hoped to entice the sharp-eyed, but always wary and suspicious, eagle. The warrior hid his horse in an aspen grove a quarter of a mile away from the pit so as not to betray his presence to any eagle that might see the tethered rabbit. Red Eagle waited the night and just before the coming of the dawn climbed into his trap to await his intended victim. Two days elapsed and Red Eagle had not been successful, but on the third morning soon after daylight, a young eagle fledging which had been unsuccessful in locating food landed on the trap to eat the rabbit and was captured by the now tired but happy warrior. He had caught the eagle by reaching up through the lattice and grabbing its legs as it sank its talons into the rabbit and tried to carry off the terrified and squalling animal.

With eagle feathers fluttering from his lance, with the head of the bird fastened on top of his head, and parts of it in his medicine bag, Red Eagle now felt invincible. Now he was mentally prepared to rid his life of the mountain man and regain in the eyes of his fellow warriors his prestige, let alone the possibility of gaining Shining Moon as his wife. With the eagle head and feathers as a totem to bolster his confidence and with vengeance as a stimulant, Red Eagle set his course up the Kooskooski River bound for the high country near the Red River hot springs. He had heard from members of Black Elk's tribe that the mountain man was taking beaver in the high country near the hot springs. He would search out the white man and take his hair to decorate his lance — decorate it as he had done with the eagle feathers.

* * *

Josh and Shining Moon had traveled back along the Nez Perce Trail to the high country near Red River with the victorious Nez Perce band of Chief Black Elk. There they separated from the band to remain in the high country where Josh would do his winter's trapping. He would trap the high country until the snow and cold drove them down the South Fork of the Kooskooski to winter quarters at Stites.

Josh had considerable success during the first three weeks of trapping and soon had half a pack (50) of beaver hides. He could now spend much more time locating good trapping areas as Shining Moon performed the tedious job of stretching and scraping the beaver pelts, a chore that Josh had previously performed himself. With all of this help, Josh ranged much further from camp in his search for productive beaver habitat.

Although Shining Moon now had a young son to care for, the child proved to be no deterrent to her productive efforts as the baby was strapped in a backpack board and was carried on her back at all times, except when she was feeding or caring for him.

Shining Moon knew that while trapping, their camp would be moved continuously and she had cached their tipi near the hot springs, to be retrieved as they were forced out of the high country by the cold and heavy snow. The weather, however, had been mild and only a little snow had fallen. If the mild weather held, there would possibly be another month of open water for trapping before the freezeup.

With one half of a pack of beaver already put away, Josh spent many of the daylight hours enjoying the camp life and playing with his young son. He was as happy as he had ever been in his whole life. He had a beautiful wife who made his life meaningful and he had a young son who would one day grow up to be a wise chief of the Nez Perce. Their needs were few, for food was plentiful and there was little to wish for. Life was a complete and total enjoyment.

It was a clear crisp morning in late November and Josh had just moved his camp to the headwaters of Bridge Creek the day before. He had found in his scouting what seemed to be a large colony of beaver and had the evening before set his six traps in the places long experience told him he would probably catch a beaver or two. He had arisen from his bed before daylight and had kissed his sleeping wife on the forehead and headed for his trapline.

The location of his sets proved to be productive for by the time he had lifted his six traps he had five large beaver. Josh was elated for with luck like this he could end his trapping and return to winter camp much sooner than he had anticipated. A pack of beaver would be more than enough to satisfy his needs for another year. Josh skinned out the last of the five beaver and had stuffed the hides in his possibles bag and was in the process of resetting his sixth trap when a chill went up his back and he cocked his head in the direction of camp. Although he was a good half mile from it, his acute hearing had picked up the sound of what he took to be the battle cry of an Indian warrior.

Apprehension gripped the mountain man as he listened intently for any further sounds and hearing none, he dropped the trap, picked up his Hawken rifle, and ran as fast as he could, yet cautiously, toward camp. As he neared its vicinity, he looked for signs of movement, and, staying in the trees, he circled the camp which had been located in a grove of aspen trees. He watched the horses and Midnight, the mule, which were still tethered in the meadow. The mule was looking in his direction, but showed no particular sign of distress. The three horses were busily cropping the partially brown bunchgrass.

Josh watched camp for a time and not seeing any movement, wondered why Shining Moon had not gotten up and built a cooking fire. She would usually arise soon after he left to check his trap line, as soon as there was light enough to do the early morning chores.

After a wait of about fifteen minutes and still not seeing any movement in camp, Josh walked slowly, every sense alert, through the trees until he could see the bed roll and note that the buffalo robe had been thrown back and exposed the immobile bodies of his wife and child. Anger and sorrow coursed through his body and casting aside all caution, he ran into the camp and threw himself onto the lifeless forms of Shining Moon and his unnamed son. He wept openly for what had been yesterday a life of extreme joy had suddenly turned into one of consuming sorrow.

How long he lay there he was not sure for he lost all track of time for sorrow so consumed him. That day turned into night and night into day before he arose from the bed and looked about him. His life now seemed to be in shambles and his only thoughts were of revenge.

Josh buried the bodies of his wife and child in a cedar grove beneath the tall straight trees which reached upward toward the celestial body for which his wife had been named.

He now searched the area around the camp and soon found evidence of the intruder. He found the moccasin tracks of one man and following these discovered the place where a horse had been tethered. The track was cold but not so cold that an expert tracker could not follow it. Assembling his equipment and taking with him only those items that he needed for fast travel, he cached his furs and other trapping equipment and with only his horse and Midnight, the mule, he set off on the trail of the assassin. With vengeance in his heart, he would pick out and destroy the killer of the only things in his life that really mattered to him, his wife and his son.

At the outset, the trail was one of a man fleeing in haste as if he were an animal. A man showing no effort to conceal the direction in which the travel was directed. It was a trail without forethought or knowledge of where he was headed, only the effort to put as much distance between him and the dastardly deed he had committed, and to do so as quickly as possible.

After following the trail for only a short distance, Josh found the head of an eagle through which had been strung a rawhide cord. Josh picked it up and thoughts ran through his mind. While the head of an eagle could belong to many warriors, he could think of only one man in the land of the Nez Perce who would want to kill him. That man was Red Eagle, son of Chief Cut Nose of the Potlatch tribe of the Nez Perce.

The direction that the trail was leading also told him that the assassin was probably a person who was native to the country, for the fleeing man was traveling west and later north back toward the Nez Perce country. The trail headed toward the high country and climbed up to the divide between the Selway and the south fork of the Kooskooski.

It was near Anderson Butte that Josh found the trail to become erratic and show signs that the Indian's horse had gone lame. The horse had apparently fallen on the icy rocks and had suffered an injury. Josh spurred his Appaloosa stallion onward, feeling now that the distance between him and this now on foot Indian could be closed more rapidly.

Night found Josh crossing the saddle between the drainages of Horse Creek and Timber Lake Creek. The trail had become only a few hours old for the retreating Indian was now walking and two feet of snow had slowed him as he led his very lame horse. Josh camped for the night in the timber near a small mountain meadow on the windward east side of the saddle. He slept only fitfully during the night and watched the sky for signs of clouds which might bring snow that could obliterate the now hot trail. Vengeance had not deranged the mind of the mountain man so much that he was not cautious. The Indian who had killed his wife and child would possibly become desperate and might double back on his trail to try to learn if anyone was following him.

Night passed uneventfully and the cold clear dawn found Josh following the trail along the divide between the South Fork and the Selway River drainages and he was now traveling generally north. From a high point in the trail, he could see that ahead the country had flattened out into a large high mountain meadow to the north and east of which the terrain dropped off rapidly to the valley of the Selway River. He was approaching Buck Meadow and would need to be cautious as the country opened up on either side of the trail for a considerable distance. The trail he was following through the two feet of snow now swung to the east through the meadow that lay on the divide between Falls Creek and Horse Creek, both tributaries of the Selway River. He was cautious. It would be here in the sparsely-timbered fringes of the meadow that one beleaguered might await a pursuer. Josh left the trail that continued on through the meadow and traveled slowly in the timber on the downwind side and along the fringe of the meadow. He watched intently a two acre island of timber in the middle of the meadow which lay about 200 yards into the center of the field. The timber and brush in the island were thick and would make an excellent place to set up an ambush for anyone wanting to watch the approaches to a camp from all directions. Although the tracks in the snow appeared to circle the island, Josh looked beyond it for a trail leading out of the timber patch and could not see any from his vantage point.

The trapper decided to circle the meadow and learn if there were tracks leading out of the meadow at any point. He stayed well back in the fringe timber and completely circled the meadow and could find no tracks leaving the meadow. Apparently his adversary was holed up in the island of timber!

Josh speculated on how he could approach the grove without exposing himself and he could not figure out a way of doing so, unless in some manner he could determine where in the island his enemy might be located. He continued to watch intently the island, the birds, and the animals for any unusual movements. He listened to the squirrels, trying to decide whether their barking betrayed the position of the hiding Indian.

Then first it was a trotting coyote which came out of the timber at the east end of the island, then two ruffed grouse that flew up and sailed with set wings to the fringe timber near his general vicinity.

Josh chose this time to run the 200 yards to the west end of the grove. He reached it without drawing a shot and then began the stealthy stalk through the island seeking his intended victim.

The sun had not as yet reached its zenith above the horizon when Josh slowly and as silently as possible — progressing only after he had examined every tree and bush before him — moved through the grove. Always he tried to keep a tree between him and any open area directly ahead. His thoughts were consumed by his concentration on this quest as he watched for the signs of the presence of anyone. The day was still and hardly a leaf moved. There was little snow under the umbrella of trees and the limbs of the evergreen trees were bent down by the weight of the snow.

The weather was cold — the temperature well below freezing. Josh could feel only a faint movement of air on his face as he moved eastward, but there was enough of a breeze that he caught the scent of horse and intermixed with it the scent of a red man. He had the advantage of the wind and his presence would be known to his adversary only when and if he caught sight of him.

And then to Josh's ear came a sound, the swish of brush rubbing against buckskin and he caught the movement of a man near the edge of trees watching the open meadow, watching for a mountain man who unbeknownst to him was watching *him*. Josh for a moment savored his position. He had recognized the red man to be Red Eagle. Thoughts of revenge flashed through his brain but caution stayed his hand and he measured the fifty or so feet between him and Red Eagle. Why should he do other than shoot down this man who had taken the lives of his most cherished wife and child. Or, should he alert the young Nez Perce and give him a chance to defend himself, an action the Indian had not done for Shining Moon.

Fair play overcame passion and Josh pulled the set trigger of his Hawken and slowly turned and started walking toward his adversary, for Josh saw that Red Eagle carried only a bow and a knife, so he chose not to shoot him with the rifle unless Red Eagle set an arrow on his bow string and tried to shoot at him.

Josh's movement caught the eye of the young Nez Perce warrior and he swung around facing the mountain man. His trepidations of the past days, that the mountain man would catch up with him, had come true. He must now face death as must every brave warrior. He had prepared himself well for just such a moment and now would come the test of this

courage, for walking slowly toward him was the huge trapper who had caused him so much misery among his fellow warriors. There before him was his chance to wipe out all of this misery as well as to count coup and stand tall among his fellow warriors.

Red Eagle saw that he was mismatched, what with only a bow and arrows against a rifle and the thought went through his mind as to why the Long Knife had not already shot him with the rifle. He felt that he must count coup against this Long Knife, even if he lost his own life. He must run up to the white man and touch him and in hand to hand combat kill him with his knife. So he did just that. He dropped his bow and reached for his knife and in almost the same motion ran at the man as hard as he could.

Josh saw the red man drop his bow and he in turn dropped his rifle and reached for his knife. He stood crouched, ready to meet the charge of the Indian. Red Eagle yelled his war cry as he charged. If he could just touch the trapper and then drive his knife deep into his chest, he would have achieved his purpose! But what if he died in the attempt? So be it, for he would walk in the hereafter as a warrior who had given his life in glorious battle.

Josh met the charge and with the agility of a cougar grasped the uplifted arm of the assailant and with superior strength forced Red Eagle to drop his knife. He then thrust his own knife deep into the chest of the Indian and felt the strength drain from the body of the warrior as he slid to the ground. Josh gazed at the body and vengeance seethed within him. He reached down and cut the scalp from the red man and stuffed it dripping with blood into his possibles bag. He was yet not vindicated, and with his knife ripped open the chest of the killer of his family and tore out his heart. He cut off a big chunk of the organ and stuffed it into his mouth and chewed. Before he was through, he had eaten raw the heart of this red man who had brought him so much sorrow.

* * *

Josh returned to his trapline and almost without being aware of what he was doing continued his trapping into the depths of winter. He soon had two packs of beaver pelts which he loaded on Midnight and with Shining Moon's pinto gelding set his course with their possessions down the South Fork of the Kooskooski River for winter camp at Stites.

He would relate the story of the death of Shining Moon and his son to Spotted Fawn and Chief Black Elk and there would be much sorrow in the camp.

Josh was to stay many years with the Nez Perce at Stites and many of these years he returned to a rendezvous to trade his pelts.